pageant
of a **woman**

by josée andrei

AMP Press 2000

A Pageant of A Woman Copyright © 1998 by Josee Andrei

ISBN 1-892453-05-3

This book was printed in Lodi, California, USA

FIRST PRINTING

Cover Design by Jennifer Durrant

I wish to express my gratitude to the friends who allowed this book to come out, my publishers, and all the friends who helped me overcome a long and difficult illness. Thank you very much.

Josée

Table of Contents

Poetry:

Pictures:

by Fred Rozendal

Josée Andrei has become a friend and fellow explorer over the last six years. She entered my life when she joined a small psychotherapy group that I was running at the Lighthouse for the Blind in San Francisco. She quickly became an important support for me when I dealt with a difficult client who was homeless and threatened to fall apart each session, I remember watching her bring him back to reality in a way that I could not, and feeling impressed. To my surprise, she wasn't annoyed with what I feared: that she might see my skill as lacking. Instead, she offered to work with me as a cotherapist. I was not open to it at the time, so she took the next step: asking to see me as a client. I debated whether there might be a conflict in our roles, especially given her talent. I felt intimidated by her confidence and my relative newness to practice, but decided to go ahead with our work. Fortunately, I did not learn until much later that she had been a therapist herself; I would have been more intimidated. Josée revealed several years after we had worked together that she immediately felt a strong connection between us from our first meeting, despite her lifelong caution in dealing with men.

Our work quickly became exhilarating and difficult. She brought intense feeling to our sessions; I contributed encouragement to use her artistic talent to explore her psyche more deeply. Later, she told me that I had offered her inspiration to expand her work in ways that had not been possible before. She is totally blind, so I was amazed when I discovered early on that she produced visual art—including painting and sculpture—in addition to verbal art—poetry and writing. In particular, I felt awe and parent-like pride when she took a winning place in a national competition sponsored by the Art Institute of Chicago, a leading museum, during our work.

In the painting that she was doing at the time, she began to use it to explore and uncover feelings and their earlier triggers by allowing herself to form images and story lines that emerged spontaneously as she painted. The paintings and in some cases sculptures and poetry provided an extraordinary medium to open her psyche up so that she could work with previously hidden conflicts and inhibitions. The result of this opening up led to a remarkable infusion of new energy into her art in turn. In therapy sessions, we elaborated and examined the images that emerged in her paintings primarily, along with their associated stories. We discovered hidden, powerful depths of meaning that spoke of her struggles, some of them occurring over the broad sweep of her life, and others of them relating directly to our relationship. A number of these images came to form major statements about our work together that we returned to them frequently to understand the larger view of our work together. For example, there was a glacier that gradually melted into water, and then many water images formed; there were prison bars separating us, but with an opening through which we could weave a tapestry; and again, a primitive temple at which she funneled spiritual energy and I expressed it in language.

Although she often attributed the unfolding of her artistic creativity to our work and I felt flattered, I did not want to repeat a mistake made by her father, which was to place her on a pedestal that served his needs. So I carefully avoided expressing my enjoyment. Also, I resonated with and understood her writing better than her painting, so I had less to say about the latter. She in turn came to think that I did not care about her art. This misunderstanding signaled the beginning of several conflicts that threatened a premature ending to our work.

On my part, I went through the ending of a very intense love relationship, feeling fragile and needing to be valued. Josée often became the most clearly positive and supportive voice amidst the din of rejection I listened to. I struggled to control my need for validation so that it did not take away from her work. On her part, she felt that I was too distant, not realizing how difficult my struggle was; she thought I was uncaring. At one time, Josée stopped her work with me for several months. Somehow we found our way through the conflicts, using them to go deeper in our work together.

In our work together, and in work alone, Josée elaborated her images into stories often, sometimes capturing past events in her life, sometimes creating fantasies that symbolically expressed her feelings and exploration. These helped her understand herself in the present. She has published several of these stories in a previous book of hers. Early on in our work she stated forcefully that she saw no use in examining her past; however, she was willing to oblige me in looking at it eventually. After much uncovering and exploration, she became more of a friend to her past. Then one day she called and said that she had broken a bone in her leg and was unable to move for an extended period. In her characteristic optimism and energy, she decided to use the time for a new creative venture: to my surprise, it was to record the stories from her life that had shaped her. Later, as I read them for the first time, I was startled as I realized that there was much that we had not talked about; she had expanded her review beyond our work together. Also I felt a new sense of wonder for life in Europe, a continent I loved but have experienced only rarely. I saw that we had gradually formed a collaborative venture, rather than a distrustful alliance. We have come to acknowledge our differences rather than to see them as a point of conflict. She has often told of how important our mutual journey has been to her, which made the struggles more tolerable for me.

I have been amazed at her increasing creativity and energy, turning to new realms as well as familiar ones. I had known of her painting, sculpting, and writing earlier. Now I gradually discovered many new expressions of her creativity: the stringing of medieval beads; recordings of music (including the lyrics and instrumentation); conducting psychological seminars in Europe, the US, and Canada; talking before various groups here and abroad; presenting shows in Europe and the US; and advising friends and strangers, among others. She has increasingly been in demand, which is a far cry from a decade ago when she left all behind in Belgium and landed in San Francisco without knowing anyone.

This book gives an inside view of her journey, often in metaphorical terms. She starts with her beginnings in an unusual location, the island of Corsica, and proceeds through France and Belgium before coming to the US. I enjoyed "tasting" the flavor of locations in Europe that I have visited, but never experienced from the inside as a resident. The second half of her book describes anecdotes from more current events in her life.

As I listen to her, in her book and in person, I hear hope and joy in aging. She started life over in her middle 50s, after having built a therapy practice and community in Europe. Now at 75, she is more energetic than many middle age adults that I know. For me, she presents a model of how I wish to mature, in the face of difficulty as well as success. I believe that her book and her life can offer hope to her readers, as well as the pleasure of listening to colorful tales.

Bon voyage!

{ *Prelude in F Major* }

How many times did you ask?
Oh my friends
How many times could I listen to you?
But tonight
I hear your voices
Light or curious
Persistent sharp
Soft whispering
Talking loud
I hear your voices
Write the story of your life
Tell us the story of your life

Meandering river from the source to the sea
Fast slow light heavy
With bridges of love
Cascades of sorrow
Ponds of happiness
Memories
Echoes

For you all I laugh
This is my heart show
Bubble dance of glass beads
Transparent or with brilliant colors
Or black or white or gray
Different skills in different keys
Measures tempos notes and poses
Symphony in F major
Friendship freedom fun and folly

The flower of wisdom that you have shown me
In one day to be born be grown and then die
All day long I am I.

1

{ *The Winter Baby* }

My parents came to their little mountain village of Moïta in Corsica in order to settle down, at least for a while. But they had a hard time finding the little nest of their dreams. There weren't any empty houses and the village was already covered with snow. Finally my father found a house at the highest part of the village that had been empty for a long time. People said it was haunted and he laughed.

My mother remained silent. Burdened with a three year old boy and her advanced pregnancy, Antoinette was tired and passive. Later she told me that she had been afraid beyond fear. They moved in at the end of November on a cold, snowy day. Could the little baby sheltered in the womb feel the anxiety of her mother?

I was born there a week before Christmas Eve, long before day break while a blizzard was raging, with no doctor or midwife.

"She's in pain. Go get Félicité," they said.

"The witch?"

"It doesn't matter. She used to be a midwife. Go quick."

The snow was high under a starry sky and in the witch's arms I began to breathe and cry.

For three months I cried all night long. The night full of sounds. Do I remember my father carrying me outside on the back balcony wrapped up in a blanket with a hot water bottle and sleeping alone in my baby carriage? Vagrant cats fighting, dogs howling at the moon, and the baby warm warm warm and frightened? Do I remember the terror?

{ Alien }

Hold me high in your arms
I want to caress the top of the trees
My father laughed
Little girl dropped from the moon
Where did I land?
By a mountain stream
Among frogs water weeds and night cries
Little spirits around
White butterflies
Looking for new shelters
There I landed in my father's arms
with a plumage of moonbeams
And gushing from my eyes
Tears of joy in glass crystal
Colored in nocturnal voices
Red and scarlet red
And fire in the sky
Constellations circling the mountains
Was it winter?
A baby a baby
A little girl dropped from the moon.

{ *A Little Girl Dropped From The Moon* }

My grandmother bent over the cradle saying, "But she can't see. She can't see." My father stared at her and then took me in his arms.

"Incredible. It's taken us three months to know." He looked into my eyes for a long time. "She's so beautiful - a little girl dropped from the moon - that's why."

My mother often talked to me about my childhood, especially about the times I couldn't remember. One time my parents went on a business trip, leaving me with Grandma. "Be sweet to her," my father said as he put me in her arms, "Good-bye."

Grandmother took a big bucket, sunk my head under water, and held it for a long time. I was struggling. I was drowning. I was dying. One of my youngest aunts came into the room. Soon I was breathing again on a young woman's bosom, soft as a feather pillow. Love was coming back. I was there alive, a baby, a three month old infant. Do I remember?

When I was 45 I was practicing in a group doing a technique called Mental Dynamics with a Belgian psychologist and friend, Marie-Claire Lefevre. As I was being regressed, I found myself as an infant drowning in a bucket. I felt my grandmother and was terrified! When I came home I called my Aunt Rose in Corsica. We had always been very close. She recounted the story and told me, "Nobody knew this except your parents." These events had never been told to me before.

I was nine months old when I began to walk. They said, "She's a tornado, a hurricane." I was always voicing, smelling, grabbing, tasting, biting, and splashing the energy of life.

There was a hearth in the middle of the room, an ancient fireplace of square construction made of brick, stones, and earth. Not easy to describe because this kind of fireplace doesn't exist anymore. Within, the wood crackled in red flames projecting the long shadows of evening on the walls. Above the flames was a cauldron of boiling water suspended from the ceiling by iron chains.

A ritual took place in spring, probably Easter time. I remember the bells, the people coming into the house. It was night, the air still and crisp. I wore a white dress made of soft wool. Everybody seemed so happy even though we were saying good-bye. We were leaving our Corsican village.

My grandfather took me in his arms and drew a cross over my forehead. "God bless the baby. God bless the baby." He began to pass me around. Everybody kissed my hair, drew a cross over my forehead and prayed, "God bless the baby. God bless the baby." It was warm and bright. "God bless the baby." I was 16 months old but I remember well everyone's unique smell, and the feeling of circling the room like a little bird.

Everyone was there but the witch. She wasn't invited. But why not? After all, hadn't she saved my mother's life - and mine as well?

{ *The Journey* }

My father used to sing a children's song:

Il etait un petit navire
Qui n'avait jamais ja jamais navigué...

Oh, once there was a little boat
a white little boat upon the blue Mediterranean Sea.

The boat we got on was huge and crowded, full of strange noises, filled with new sounds, strong odors, salty mists. People had brought their own food - bread and cheese, hard boiled eggs, and many things I had never eaten. Some were drinking wine. Some were getting sick. In that boat, with all those grownups together, it didn't smell very good. Yet, there was something nice about it.

Many of the passengers were playing guitar, mandolin, and accordion, some singing, some dancing, some whistling. Above all, the stillness of night spread its woolly blanket over the moving ship. We had only chaise lounges to lie on. I was listening to the chant of the sea, feeling the boat rocking, rocking, rocking. Deep within me I heard the lullaby - *Il etait un petit navire...* I closed my eyes and fell asleep with a content heart.

In the morning I found myself sitting with my parents in a café, where by custom, patrons called the waiters by knocking on the glasses with their teaspoons. People were talking to me and I became aware that I could understand many of their words. Suddenly a woman shouted in surprise, "Oh, the little girl is blind. She can't see." I felt

6

people turning their faces towards me. I felt their eyes upon me. It was hot, hot and scary. For the first time I intuitively realized they could see the world with their eyes. I could only see its shadows.

From that day I knew that all my life I would have to illuminate everything with my mind. That's why that day I changed the glass concert café into a sparkling crystal rain. That day sound and light combined their vibrations to fill my body with joy. My mouth tasted it. My skin touched it. I heard it. I smelled it. Did I see it? How was it? Water and fire together surging from a fountain of pink marble.

{ *Sounds* }

Sitting still
Listening
Is it my breath
the wind?
A fine perception
Makes my heart resound
In tom-tom vibration
Raindrops on the roof
Voices
Footsteps
Engines
Sirens
The throbbing of life
If I go over
Behind into
I may dive
Into the silence
Silence
Silence
And there a deep note
Your voice
In harmony
With the universe
In me.

{ *Holidays Of Defiance* }

All the village was dressed in snow. We had returned for Christmas and I was going to be six years old. I didn't know much about Christmas except that it was a time of celebration. Was it the new scents, new flavors, new sounds, new pleasures? They killed a pig down in the shed - all those screams and an acrid odor as they singed the hair. Then the men came into the house with enormous buckets full of blood.

"We are going to make boudin, a blood sausage," they announced. I felt sick. I rushed outside into the snow and ran next door to Félicité's house. My mother had told me many times, "I don't want you to go to the witch's. She's going to cast a spell on you. You won't learn anything good there." But I went anyway and loved it.

I pushed her door open and the dampness and darkness of the house fell heavily over my shoulders. Felicite was there. She dressed in the style of the old country women, a long black dress with a black handkerchief partially covering her long grey hair. She was sitting in front of her wooden stove trying to keep herself warm. Was she waiting for me?

"Hey come in, Little Pudding. You sure have the complexion of a city girl," she said, handing me a slice of orange, which at the time was quite a delicacy. "Seems that they killed a pig at grandma's this morning, huh?"

"Yes, they did. I couldn't stand it. I think it's gross. It smelled like the time that I burned the tip of my hair with a candle, but much stronger. All those men coming into the house with blood."

"Blood is red."

"But what is red?"

"Red is fire. Red is anger," the witch explained.

"What about tears? What color are they?"

"They are clear drops of salty water. They taste almost like the sea."

"Then we heard the bells toll. "Our neighbor died," she said.

"Died? But we don't die."

"No, you're right little girl. We don't die. We go to heaven."

"No, we don't go to heaven. We come back again."

"That's nonsense, little girl."

"No, it's not nonsense. I know in my heart that I am going to be reborn. It's that way."

"Have you- ever heard the voice of the devil?"

"Who is the devil?"

"The powerful evil."

"I don't understand."

"I may let you hear it. Would you like to?"

I was burning with curiosity. I vividly recall the room, the floor made of grossly cut planks, loosely nailed together. Just down the room was a little barn expelling a light smelling vapor. She pulled up one of the planks.

"Put your head here and listen". I listened and listened. Suddenly, hearing a bleating, a harsh and deep cry, I backed off, frightened. "Close the hole. Please close the hole". I can smile today. You got me witch. All of my childhood the cry of a billy goat was for me the voice of Satan.

In the evening I went with my mother to see Nanny, a woman who sewed dresses for all the women in the family. We came to show her a beautiful piece of silky material. "I need a beautiful gown for Finau, (a nickname given to me by my family). My sister's wedding is in two weeks". Nanny took the piece of fabric, spread it over the table, and ironed it out. She took my measurements, stroked my hair, yawned, and said that the gown would be ready in one week.

Mother took me by the hand and we went outside. I felt strange and said, "Mama, I don't think that Nanny is going to have the dress ready in a week."

"Why do you say that?"

"Because I think she is going to die."

My mother was shocked. She slapped my face hard. "Forget that. Never say that again." Three days later Nanny was dead. I never had my face slapped that hard before or after. I felt ashamed that I may have done something very wrong.

"I don't want you to go to the witch's ever again", my mother said. The witch? Did the witch tell me that Nanny was going to die? Who told me that Nanny was going to die? I felt it. I didn't know why.

That same evening I got lost above the village. It was very late. Three boys came to me. "Where's Paul", they asked.

"My brother?"

"Tell us. Where is your brother." Just then they saw him. They took him and tied his hands and feet with a thick rope and began to hit him asking, "Why didn't you do to your sister what we said?" They tortured him and he was screaming.

"Yes, yes, I will do it. I will do it." And then I found myself on the ground. Was I drowning again? I lost consciousness.

Later, my brother led me home through the narrow street. I was crying. And then I heard the billy goat. It was my sixth birthday. Was it the dark ritual of Satan?

{ Ribbons Of Solitude }

My parents were leaving us with Grandma again and I was frightened. "We are going to Paris to look for a job and a nice house", they said to my brother. "Watch the top of the mountains carefully. When you see the snow melting and flowers springing from the earth, it will be spring and we will come to get you".

I wished I could stay with my paternal grandmother, Angelle, but she was very sick. I remember her and Grandfather Mathias. They had a very beautiful house with a salon and they read books. I was really impressed. And each time I went, Julia, the maid, made delicious desserts for me, such as flan, apple pies, and butter cookies. And they bought me nice shoes and clothes. But when I was back at Grandma Mathy's I couldn't wear them. "The snobs bought you this", she would say.

A Woman Named Yesterday

Sitting at her window
A hair pin between her teeth
She fastens her last braid
Coils it around her head
The hair pin exactly where she wants it.

She looks at a flock of grey pigeons
Flying over the distant horizon
Idle in her expectancy
As the morning flows by.

Yesterday is gone
Keeping all her reflections in her heart
The window is closed
Forgotten memories shimmer
In the summer sun behind the glass.

We were a bunch of cousins living together; neglected, going barefoot, and not always very clean. Grandma yelled all the time at the top of her voice, swearing and cursing. She was obese, I could feel this as she heavily dragged her feet across the floor. When she sat the chairs would creak loudly. She was harsh and hateful, trying to keep me away from the other children. "She can't see. She can't run. She can't…"

But the kids didn't care. They were wild and free, leaping over streams, playing in the woods, camping in the trees. With them holding my hand I could run, and maybe in a way I *could* see.

But as much as she could, Grandma kept me home sitting by the fire on the wooden bench, alone. She would bring me thick slices of black bread spread with lard and large bowls of milk with lots of sugar that she forced me to eat and drink. Maybe she wanted me to be fat just like her.

Many times the children helped me to escape. We would play all day long in the woods and had fun until we had to go back to the house where I would get punished.

One rainy morning we got bored and I suggested that we go visit Grandfather Mathias. He was alone now. Grandmother Angelle had died in the winter after many years of pain.

"Welcome kids. I have plenty of Jesus candy for you today", and from his pocket he withdrew the little white, pink, and blue sugar candy shaped as baby Jesus that we were fond of. "You can play in the house. But don't jump on the couch with your dirty feet. I have some work to do. Be good". He retired into his bedroom.

Crowding around the fireplace we tried to make up games and finally decided to do something very strange,- to make caramel. We sneaked into the kitchen looking for sugar, water, butter, and a big pot that we set over a fire, stirring and stirring until the whole thing started to boil.

"Now, now we have to pour the caramel onto something cold."

"What about the marble mantle piece?"

And so we did.. The caramel began to thicken. I was the youngest and I cried. "I want some. I want some.'

"No, it's too hot."

"I want it right now!"

Hortencia took a big piece of it with her spoon and put it in my mouth. It was fire itself and I screamed. We heard Grandfather Mathias coming and we ran. He chased us for a while and we were all scared. Then the other kids disappeared in the town square and I slowly walked home alone.

When I got there I heard Grandfather Philippe singing in his workshop. I came in and sat on the floor and told him about the adventure of the caramel. "Nobody apologized to Grandfather Mathias? Who's going to clean up the mess?"

I felt ashamed. I felt myself so small with tiny hands. "I will, Grandpa, I will."

"I don't mean little you", he smiled. "Forget that adventure. Tomorrow if you want I will show you the secret spring. But I will have to wake you very early in the morning. We have to go down to the valley and up to the next mountain. I will give you Maura, the black donkey to ride. I will take the mule and we will be connected by rope."

14

My mouth was still sore from the hot caramel. "Grandfather, can I have some water from the secret spring?" He poured me a glass from a large jug. I drank it and felt at peace.

The first trip to the spring enchanted me totally. The donkey, solidly roped to the mule was going steadily, up and down through roots, rocks, fallen trees, and ditches of water. Grandfather Philippe was a quiet man. He didn't talk much. But once in a while he would encourage me with his song, while gently handing me flowers and branches to show me the first manifestation of springtime.

Then we stopped. Surging from underground between two tall rocks, the spring was bubbly and warm. I drank and drank insatiably.

We sat on the grass and had a frugal breakfast of hard boiled eggs, breads, cheese, and dried fruit in silence. After we ate, Grandfather Philippe taught me the names of the birds according to their song; the names of the wildflowers according to their composition on the stem, their center, their corolla, their petals, and the sweetness or bitterness of their fragrance.

Over the next few months he taught me how to recognize stones: granite, quartz, silex, serpentine. He taught me how to talk to the trees and how to hear the varied voices of the water; running, flowing gently, quiet, dormant, and changing with the seasons. He taught me so many things.

One day in the summer I asked, "Grandpa, why don't you take some of the other kids to the secret spring?"

"They are as exuberant as poppies. They don't know how to listen yet. Someday I will take some of them. Now it is your time to listen to the nature talk."

{ Paris, The Rose }

Each time the man visited my mother she would say to me, "Go out, play in the backyard. We have some things to do in the house." It was always on the day my father came late from work.

The man would always bring me a huge box of chocolate cookies, "All for you, my little girl." I didn't like him. "Can't you say 'thank you' to Uncle Minotelli?" I tightened my face, accepted the bribe disgracefully, ran across the yard, reached the little alley between two buildings and threw the cookies into the well. But I kept the box. I knew the cardboard wouldn't melt and people would find out when they came to draw fresh water.

I knew he was tall, his voice was coming from high above me. I thought he was a giant. What frightened me at times, I never exactly remembered his name, so in the secret of my heart I called him *tagliatello,* - noodle. His footsteps were light, we would hardly hear him coming, his voice like caramel, soft and sticky. "Here's your treat, little one." They never could get me to smile or say "thank you".

On those days I felt lonely with the other children in school. And with my mother and the man inside the house, I felt rejected, ostracized, abandoned. But I was usually content to play by myself in the backyard, planting a garden around the horse chestnut tree, making wooden toys, and remembering Grandfather Philippe's talks and teachings.

My parents were opera lovers. Almost every Saturday my mother dressed me up and took me with them. My brother, Paul, was lucky. He could stay home and play. Some evenings I would long for my toys, for my bed, for the silence of my room. But alone with my brother I would have been terrorized. With my parents I was safe.

I could fall asleep while the music was playing. But once in a while my father would pat my shoulder waking me up, "Listen to this aria full of sorrow; to Werther calling for death; to La Traviatta dying and abandoned; to Rigoletto crying over his dying daughter." Was it really a rich cultural experience for a seven-year-old child? I would say, yes. I developed a kind of love/hate relationship with the opera. As a teenager I began to listen to Verdi, Wagner, and Mozart. Then I became infatuated with Carmen. I bought records. I learned arias. I dressed like a gypsy. I played. I sang. I danced. I cried. It was great fun. Thank you, Mr. Bizet.

My parents were also very fond of carnivals. At that time in Paris we had many of them, mostly neighborhood carnivals. But in the springtime during the month of May and in the fall during the month of September we went to the great carnivals with friends and neighbors. My father was always lucky, winning candy, cakes, dolls, stuffed animals, bottles of wine and cheap champagne.

It was mostly on Saturday night that my parents invited the neighbors to share the sweet trophies. I didn't want to be included, but then again, I didn't want to miss some of their mysterious conversations, in spite of the fact that those people were so loud,- joking, singing stupidly, drinking, eating, and incessantly waltzing.

Once, my father got me up on a table, trying to make me dance and sing. "She's good. She has a beautiful voice. And she knows so many steps." Everybody gathered around. "Hey bravo, little one. Sing and dance."

But I began to cry. Then I was sobbing. "I want to sleep. I want to go to bed. I'm tired. I want to sleep." My father took me in his arms and carried me into my bedroom, closed the door and left.

Carnivals are noisy and smelly and crowded, I thought. But then I liked the merry-go-round. I could catch the bell sometimes and win a free ride. I liked the ponies, the music, the caramel apples, the *beignets*, and the cotton candy. But did I like the carnivals? I wasn't so sure.

It was during one of them that this unfortunate incident occurred. My parents stopped at a game table. They were playing numbers. I got bored and fell asleep with my chin resting on the edge of the table. I wanted to leave and touched the people on either side of me. I thought they were my parents.

"What do you want child?" said a cold voice.

"I want to leave."

"Oh, you can leave and go."

"No, I want to leave with Papa and Mama."

"Are your parents here?"

"Yes, they are here. They were here. I don't know now."

I began to cry and wandered into the crowd. I was alone and didn't know where I was going. I felt lost and cried louder, and I thought, "The gypsies are going to get me, like Remy in my story book." The gypsies had stolen him and made him work in the circus on dangerous things like learning to walk on ropes and jump. And he never found his parents again.

A woman put her arms around me. "What happened little girl? Are you lost?"

"My parents are gone. I don't know where they are."

"Come with me to the public address system."

I heard a voice calling out over the loudspeaker, "Josée, a little girl with short brown hair and a pink dress is waiting for her parents at the entrance."

My father arrived first, shortly after the announcement. And then my mother. They didn't pay much attention to me. They began to argue on and on about what happened and who was to blame. I didn't speak. I felt embarrassed, then angry, and I stopped crying. Maybe I would be better off with the gypsies. Growing up I could learn to tame the tigers and lions and play with the dogs and the monkeys.

Sitting quietly in the metro I began to count the stations. Fourteen before getting off. And then we would walk three blocks before arriving at my parents' home, or was it also mine? At times the house was silent. I played alone, never bored, always making up new games, inventing new toys with everything I could gather, pieces of wood, wire, rocks, broken porcelain.

But in the evening everybody came over to our place and the house was suddenly alive with people from all over Europe, political fugitives, they said. There was my family. I belonged to the place, to the warm place where I was praised and loved, well dressed and well fed. Free to express, to come and go. But some of the time I was an orphan, a stranger, the little ugly duckling. Different, misunderstood, alone. Was it already the cage, the trap?

I can picture myself as a nine-year-old child walking along the Seine in a yellow dress among the florists, book sellers, peanut vendors; skipping upon the Surrenne Bridge; breathing the scent of the river through the air of an accordion; being treated by some young women of the neighborhood like their little sister, or perhaps like a doll as they combed my hair and took me to the *grand magazin* to buy cheap

19

perfume and paper roses.

Riding the escalator was one of my favorite amusements. I enjoyed observing people passing, rushing through a palette of odors,- coffee, leather, fabrics, cleaning products, fruit, crayons, fresh bread, chocolate, cheeses, meat,- more than my nose could ever sense. It was my way of looking through the kaleidoscope of life. Street cars passing, the street always full of strange noises, vendors, street barkers, the mailman the milkman, the baker, the kids playing on the sidewalk. It was very pleasant to be a city girl.

We lived in what they called the Red District, not far from the Renault factory. I heard people saying big words: communist, anarchist, fascist. I tried to understand. We had guests all the time from Italy and Germany. They were always talking, especially during dinner and I pretended to fall asleep and let myself slide under the table. They were all so excited they forgot about me. I don't have enough ears to listen to what they are saying, I thought. I felt my brain expanding, expanding...

I recall when the Spanish man moved into the little shack at the far end of the backyard. Louis became my father's friend. I loved him with all of my heart. Soon he became ill. Everyday my mother sent me to visit Louis with hot food and toasted bread. "Be brave. Don't stop to play with the other children now. He's waiting for his meal."

He would talk to me in a very strange way. "Together, tomorrow we will conquer the right to be treated as human beings." Sometimes he would give me a fruit called a pomegranate, *"la granada"* the fruit of revolution. What does he mean? How can he be so sure of what tomorrow will bring? I didn't understand. But I was listening, listening, listening, again, again, and again. Then, during the Christmas holidays, Louis died.

20

February came, the Riot, the great day, they said. A man was shot just in front of our house. People brought him in. They called an ambulance, but he died. I remember the barricades, the cries of hatred, and Paris the Rose coated in blood.

I Don't Remember

They brought the man's body into the backyard
I don't remember his name
Was he a friend, a stranger?
Everyone there kept saying "Shot on the barricade"

It seemed something shocking
Unbelievable
They talked
I don't remember their words
They milled around
I don't remember where they went

It must have been a rainy day
February in Paris is always gray
But I can't remember
Absence of memories makes the heart lonely
Absence of memories makes for survival.

{ *The Southern Side Of The Cube* }

This first image of Marseilles remains forever in the well of my memory. Paradise Street in August - it sounds like a pop song. No, it was only the hottest spot in the heat, a laboratory of disintegration. Dusty and violent with brown kids in tattered clothes, whores pacing the sidewalk, sailors in brothels, charged with the smell of deprivation and the scent of the sea. That was Paradise Street.

Our apartment on the first floor was minuscule and cramped. "We are going to move from here very soon", my father promised. "Don't walk on the street for no reason." We left after two months, but it seemed to me that we stayed for two years, ten years, or maybe an entire lifetime.

One day I spoke to my father, "You have taught me so much. I am a very well-read person, but I don't know how to read. I want to go to school to learn how to read and write."

"The only place that you can go is a boarding school for blind girls. Would you like to be away from us, live with strangers, sleep in a dormitory?"

"Yes, yes." And I told myself, "I want to be away from Paul. I am growing up. I am turning into a young woman. What is going to become of me if I don't go to school?" I fought and I won. For the first time I experienced my power.

{ *The Time Of Abundance* }

I remember my first day at the special education boarding school. It was the only one in town and it was run by nuns. I came into the chapel. It was quiet with a strong scent of flowers and candles spread everywhere. I felt lightly dizzy, found a church bench, and knelt. I put my head in my hands and fell asleep. Someone stroked my hair gently. Startled, I stood up quickly. It was the nun in charge of the chapel.

"What are you doing here my child? Are you new at the school?"

"Yes, Sister." I was embarrassed.

"Come with me. I'm going to show you around."

"We have three superimposed gardens. The first, on flat ground, is for short breaks. The second, above the rocky stairs, is for longer recesses. There is a surging fountain, a reproduction of the Grotto of Lourdes that encloses a statue of Notre Dame and St. Bernadette."

"What a strange language", I thought, "would my father laugh? I don't dare ask any questions."

"This is the third garden. We keep it for picnics, sports, processions, rituals. There is a big lawn and plenty of little paths for fun. We also have several kinds of unusual flowers in the back and a little house for the sisters' novitiate. I'm sure you are going to love it. But now let's go meet the other girls. They are just finishing the rosary."

"The what?"

"The rosary. You don't know my child? You will learn soon. The rosary is made of beads. On each bead we repeat a prayer to the Virgin Mary, our mother. It's like offering her a flower each time. We ask her to protect us, to help us during our lifetime, and to save us from evil."

In my memory I saw the witch and heard the billy goat.

What is the Soul

What is the soul?
Where is the soul?

I don't ask for the answer
Sing me your life.

I enjoyed my small bed of shiny metal, my space surrounded by cotton curtains, my personal locker. I quickly made new friends and became a good student, and also at times, a trouble maker.

After the first week of school, I was asked if I wanted to do my communion. "What is it? Explain it to me."

"Five other girls are going to do it, too. They will tell you."

I was puzzled and questioned the girls.

"Say yes and don't worry. It's a lot of fun", they explained. "We are going to wear long white muslin dresses, a long white veil, a crown of roses, and there will be candles, flowers, and beautiful songs during the ritual. Everything will be white. Our parents will be around us."

"I don't know what my atheist father will say. I don't even know if he will come. What else do we have to do?"

"Just learn some catechisms."

"What are catechisms?"

"It's a book with questions and answers about God, Jesus, heaven, hell, and the angels. You just have to memorize it."

So in three weeks I learned all about the glory of God and the sin of man. My parents came to the mass and the big communion banquet given by the school. Everybody told us, "it's the most beautiful day of your life." But how do they know? Although it was, indeed, a day of great joy.

Quickly I learned how to read and write and I did it with greed. Hungry for knowledge, books became the celestial manna in the desert of my ignorance. My friends and I were known as the chatty glee - the insupportable philosophers, the gabbing library rats.

The winter is seldom inclement in Marseilles, but this one was snow over sleet, ice over snow and we wanted to enjoy a day off with no school. Inside there are many things to do for teenage girls - read, listen to music, sing carols, play pop songs on the piano, dance and talk.

"I don't want to sit at a desk", said Cathy with hostility. "Let's sit on the heater. It's not that hot". There was only room for three. I sat on the floor in front of them. We started our meeting with books, politics, emotions, the fear of possible war, disenchantments and pleasures.

"My mother doesn't care about me. She's always late."

I was interrupted by loud footsteps and a heavy voice, Sister Marcelle. She was in her eighties and had been a nun since she was sixteen years old. "Please, please girls, don't sit on the heater. You know it's going to give you sensations".

We giggled without moving, but then I pulled them by the bottom of their skirts, "Hey, make room for me. It's my turn. Let me sit." This time the laughter turned into hysteria.

For three days we were separated from the entire school as punishment and I was sorry for my friends. We were forced to live in the infirmary in total silence. But they did allow us to read and write. What a great favor.

{ *Enticing Knowledge* }

My interest for literature, philosophy, humanistic sciences had begun. I was a fifteen-year-old woman, romantic and brilliant - the pride of my father or perhaps his delusion. I was stepping out of his teachings, escaping from his influence. Pygmalion lost his life purpose, and so he died.

"School is no good, neither God nor master", said Louis to my father when I was seven. But despite my father I went to school. Seven years later, Sister Helene, my French teacher, became my second mentor. I was fourteen years old. One day she said to my father, "This little girl is my pride." Was he pleased? I still doubt it today.

Dear Papa,

One day you left and I was alone. One day so long ago.

I just can't remember your voice. Sometimes I make music with drums and flute and all sorts of instruments. I sing your favorite songs in your favorite keys but I never hear you singing. Your voice has gone somewhere into the universe.

Yes, Papa. You taught me the pleasure of being alive. You showed me the value of friendship, compassion, and honesty. But also remember that you wanted to play Pygmalion. Yet I couldn't fit into your dream. I wasn't Your Fair Lady. I had dark hair, olive skin, brown eyes, and a deep voice and some obvious rebellious streaks.

But I changed. Today I am fair, and my rebellious streak has turned into a powerful personality. I wonder if intuitively you knew what kind of woman I was going to be and you were afraid of watching me grow up. I was there, already a young woman.

What did you wish for your sixteen-year-old daughter? Yes, what did you wish? Elegantly dressed, beautiful, intelligent, submissive.

One evening Louis stroked my hair and told you, "No school for this child, no god, no master." I was seven years old. But in spite of Louis and almost against your will I went to school. I knew it would be my salvation.. Some books have become my masters. And my studies became my path.

Hey, Papa. Are you listening to me from where you are? Can you hear me? Can you understand me? And myself, can I understand you better today now that you are talking to me through memories and silence.

{ *Sister Helene* }

I felt a strong attraction for Sister Helene. She was bright with a fine sense of humor. She opened up my teen years to elegance, subtlety, and spiritual awakening. During vacation time we wrote each other endless letters. She never forced me to believe anything and always showed great respect for my opinions and discoveries. Her example and her kindness inspired me.

Later, working as a therapist, I still remember how with thoughtfulness and affection she taught me a high regard for my fellow humans. I seldom found such a clean and clear heart able to modulate and harmonize assertiveness and compassion. She was alive. She laughed bubbly streams and cried crystal clear.

One night she took a small group of students to a Debussey evening. I said, "I would walk kilometers and miles and miles to listen to Debussey."

"Never mind the kilometers", she said. "We are taking the trolley."

I guess if we survive abuse, rejection, and abandonment, it is because we've met extraordinary people to help us keep the fire alive. But we are the guardians of the fire. We can change the embers into vivid flames and let the glacier melt into a lake.

Tell me, dear reader, do you ever perceive yourself as a synthesizer?

Funny, what do you mean a synthesizer? What a funny question.

Yes, couldn't you be the receptacle of all the exceptional people that you met during your entire lifetime?

Teachings

If you teach me from your head
My head gets stuck in the clouds
But if you lead me by the heart
We may follow a way to serenity.

{ The Struggle }

My brother Paul said, "Never will a man marry a blind girl. Who needs such a burden? But, since you are so beautiful, you can become a high class prostitute."

I left the kitchen and my brother and went to take a bath. I thought of him as a raja and decided to wash and separate myself from the bestiality of man.

Mirage

A glass of water for the Raja. It's so clear going down his throat. Soon he gets high. Raja's are secretive. A mind full of malignant designs. They used to drink from muddy ponds with bamboo bridges and fallen trees carrying intense feelings of uncertainty. Every morning a child sings a song, or maybe it's a bird or a clear stream and the song says, "Life, life, life, life is blue red". Life is any color you want. It's an accident or a purpose or a cycle. What is Life?

La drole de guerre, like a huge grey rat, day by day was surreptitiously gnawing on everyone's courage. Refugees began to pour incessantly along the southern roads; the defeat, the armistice, the end, perhaps the end of times; or will a new rising sun appear to regenerate our spirit? Is there hope?

Paul departed for his own adventure, careless even for his own life. His leaving didn't change anything for me. I left the boarding school and went to stay with my mother. I was alone, just as before.

Then a turning point. I went to a regular lysée and met Mlle. Tozin, my philosophy teacher and next mentor. I still like to remember the time I became friends with her. What a bright woman.

Every Friday afternoon she took me to her home where we would have a fabulous lunch. Her parents were farmers somewhere in the Pyrenees Mountains. The food was real - real butter, real bread, real cheese, and fresh vegetables soaked in rich cream. She probably saved me from debilitation and malnutrition because I stayed healthy even during the rationing time.

Even more, Mlle. Tozin opened my mind and nurtured my soul. We were playing with dangerous concepts during that dreadful era. It happens sometimes that the law of your heart, your moral law, is above the law of society. Antigone buried her dead brother in spite of the king's rule. You see how it is possible that civil disobedience can be the noblest action of the human soul.

Yes, indeed, it was the time of resistance. My mother was one of the persons working to keep the uniforms of the defeated French army in shape. She would smuggle out pants, shirts, jackets, scarves. Twice a month, on Saturday mornings, she would send me with a brown suitcase containing clothes for the men hidden in the woods. I was dressed as an angel, in a white dress with blue ribbons in my hair.

Once, I remember it was almost spring and I couldn't reach the train station. The previous night's bombing had been murderous and I didn't know where to walk. I was lost in my own town. A German soldier approached me gently, "Where are you going?"

"I am going to visit my aunt. She is sick."

"Where?" I gave the name of another village.

"The train station has been bombed. But my friend and I can use the army car and give you a ride to the next station. What are you carrying?"

"My clothes, my books. I plan to stay for two weeks," I said. But

I thought, my suitcase contains my death and they are going to open it. Are they going to torture me? Kill me? Fear began to creep into my heart. No, I can't be frightened. Antigone paid for her disobedience with her life. They won't open it. They won't.

Twenty minutes later I got on the train. From now on I will pay attention to my North Star. I sat down and the train began slowly to leave the station.

Every other Saturday I went to a little southern town called La Tour d'Aigue. There two elderly men were waiting for me with a truck loaded with hay so I could lie down comfortably without being seen. Thirty kilometers to the little village of Grambois. What a hay ride. As I reached my destination the church bell rang announcing to the men in the woods that they could come to pick up their clothes.

When I was there I stayed overnight at the priest's house with the maid and Monsieur Marcel. Monsieur Marcel was the priest's brother, a young man 28 years old, bed ridden since the age of 15. He had been injured in a football accident. Soft spoken, always gently smiling, Monsieur Marcel was the saint of the village, a role model and inspiration, and for some people, an idol. I was rather intimidated by all the crowd around him. I was relieved when they took me back to the train station after the Sunday morning mass.

{ *Evening In Blue* }

The living room table was covered with blue light bulbs; all painted with the liquid blue medicine my mother used to rub inside my throat each time I would lose my voice in a gust of mistral wind. My father picked up the light bulbs one by one and returned them to their sockets.

"Don't you think the dark blue drapes would be thick enough to obscure the windows?"

My father talked from above, "No, light can filter through every little hole. The German reconnaissance has the vision of a hawk."

I sighed, "How long is this war going to last?"

"Only God knows, if there is one", laughed my father.

My mother and I began to set the table. "Tonight we are going to have a dinner in blue." Mother seemed pleased by the idea and began to sing.

" I am lonesome tonight with all my dreams. I am lonesome tonight without your love."

Sadness gripped my heart and I growled, "Stop that mom. Aren't you tired of hearing this corny song on the radio all the time? What makes you so happy? The war?"

"The war makes me cry. But what is the use of tears?"

I put a glass on the table. "Mom, tears mean pain and sorrow. Your song is empty, it is bottomless nonsense."

Mom drew the drapes and turned on the light. "All that blue chills the house, like the frost of winter," she said.

"Yes. And it's only September third."

We felt the quiet evening failing upon us, cooking blue silence, blue sadness, blue solitude of a bride, a young mother, an older woman. Suddenly we heard the upstairs neighbor playing his harmonica. "Oh. There's that song again."

But this time the music was distant, soft, almost a murmur; a song without words; veiled, dressed in white like the image of death in the Spanish poem I was studying, "La Muerte, vestida de blanco."

I shivered, went into my bedroom and came back wrapped in a long blue shawl that had been given to me a few days before. I sat at the dining room table and my father set a dish in front of me. What was it? My mouth was too dry to taste it and I pushed it away. I felt the blue pouring from the ceiling like the omen of doom.

{ *My Friend Nina* }

Rumors were going around that Nina was sleeping with German officers. She took another path, disappeared, and I lost my friend. Was it the road of darkness?

I woke up late that Sunday morning and asked my mother, "Why do people sound so excited?"

"Did you forget? They are going to round up as many people as they can to watch the women who slept with German soldiers. They are going to shave their hair in public to punish them."

"Is Nina one of them?"

My mother remained silent and crossed the room quickly. "Let's lock the doors, close the windows, and draw the shades", she said. "We are not part of the mob."

In the evening I went to Nina's house. Her mother opened the door. "Nina is in the basement. Some friends came over, but she doesn't want to see anyone. Tonight her father is going to take her to another town."

"Please, I want to say good-bye to her. Tell her. Ask her."

She left, went downstairs, and came back. "Go say good-bye."

Nina was lying on the floor wrapped in blankets. As I entered the room I felt someone leaving, a woman. Before closing the door she spoke with a harsh voice, "Look at yourself. You had better not go carousing again."

I bent over, "Nina, Nina, I love you."

She recognized me, but her voice was weak, "Thank you, Jo. I just had an abortion. I am afraid. I hope I won't die."

"Oh, Nina. No, you won't die. Your father is going to take you away to a new life. Maybe we won't see each other again. But I won't forget you. I love you, Nina."

"Thank you, Jo. We have been good to each other. It was my best friendship. I will think of you for a long time."

Direction

I found you drifting quietly
Upon the full moon river
With you I changed my direction
Now my brain is in my flute.

Pond At Sunset - acrylic on canvas, 1994

Moon at Her Mirror - acrylic on canvas, 1996

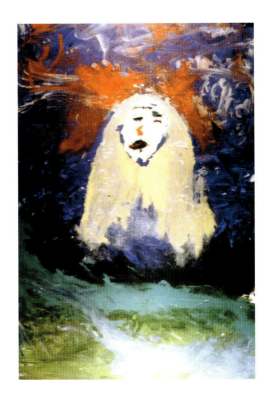

Visitations In The Twilight - acrylic on canvas, 1994

I've Been There and Back, Have You? - acrylic on canvas, 1997

40

Back home I found my mother crying. "Our Jewish friends are dead, the parents, the children…"

"… and Margaret?"

"Yes, Margaret, too."

I began to cry silently for I knew Margaret very well. She was the neighborhood nurse, appointed two years before to take charge of the dispensary. Dark, petite, always running, always talking in a juicy voice, peach and watermelon at any season of the year.

Nobody could manipulate people better than Margaret for what she called *the good cause*. Teen girls were one of her most important preoccupations. "We have to keep them out of mischief", she would say. "War time is a time of misery and dissipation."

"Listen girls", she said to us, "every Saturday you should come to give a hand at the children's day care center." Since we didn't have too much fun those days, we all went. Margaret divided us into small groups of five. Nina, Elsie, and I were her favorites. "They are quick and conscientious. I really prepare them to be leaders." Our group was assigned a special task and she put us to work in the infant section at the very end of the room.

The dispensary was housed in a kind of barracks used through the years by soldiers, hobos, and Turkish immigrants. Inside the door there was a mixture of odors - mildew, ether, ammonia. A narrow wooden door and two air holes filtered a streak of light and a tiny bit of street breeze. We were five inexpert girls undressing babies, washing them, weighing them, changing them, and dressing them again. It became our Saturday routine.

Soon, I felt burdened, dissatisfied, so I stopped going to the daycare center. I spent all my time at home reading Zola and writing poetry. My Saturday afternoons became gentle rivers smoothly crossing the tempestuous ocean of life.

One evening we were just finishing our dinner when we heard a buzz. "It's only me, Margaret", she barged in. "Brrrr, it's cold tonight."

Mother smiled, "How nice of you to pay us a visit. Sit down and get warm." "Oh, well, I just came to talk to your daughter." She stepped towards me. "Hey, Jo, why don't you come to the clinic anymore?"

"Because I don't want to. I don't like babies. They pee and poop all over your fingers."

Margaret grabbed me by the shoulders. "What do you think you did? How did you grow up? How can you talk that way about little human beings? Someday you will have babies of your own and this is an important opportunity to learn."

"No, Margaret. I will be a writer, a musician, a sailor, a fisherman... anything but a mother."

"Don't be silly, kid. Come and help raise our future patriots. Isn't it a noble thing to do?"

"No."

"Did you say 'no'? How dare you be so selfish."

A weird idea popped into my brain. "I can't do it! Look, Margaret, I am scared of babies. They wail and scream. They are gooey monsters, huge wiggly worms trying to fall from the changing table so that you can feel bad. Good for nothings."

Margaret burst into a good, humorous, Homeric laugh. "How would you like to take care of the six year old children? With your imagination you would be a terrific storyteller."

{ *Little Sarah* }

When they killed little Sarah I thought I was going to die. This is painful but I will survive.

Yellow chick with silver wings,
Gentle flower dressed in red,
Sweet, it's time to go to bed.

I hurried out of my room when I heard people loudly calling for my mother and talking to her. Why are they coming so early? What could it be? Then I heard little Sarah's voice, "Mama, where is Mama?" Some of the people were lamenting. All of them were talking in confusion. My god, I thought, this sounds like the chorus of a Greek tragedy. But I soon understood what horror and sorrow had fallen on our home and our hearts.

I listened to the people speaking. At four o'clock in the morning the German soldiers broke into the store, breaking, tearing, smashing everything they could find. They searched the house, arresting the entire family but leaving little Sarah behind, alive. She had been asleep in a corner of the attic. How could it be possible? For what reason? One never knows things, the strange mystery of human destiny.

Sarah stayed with us for several months, sheltered, fed, loved. Little sister escaped from hell. In those days there wasn't any time for regrets or procrastination. We thought she was safe. We forgot.

Everyday she would play in the backyard for a short while but we could never take her outside. Then we heard more bad news about the Gestapo arresting Jews and torturing people. My mother packed Sarah's belongings. The next morning, on Sunday, we took a trip to the countryside where some friends of ours lived in a little village. Sarah would stay there until the end of the war. There she would be happier. She could spend her time outside, free in the sunshine, and play with the other kids on the sidewalk. She was always smiling, laughing, dancing, singing little songs. We visited her almost every Sunday. Was it a mistake?

One afternoon while the kids were playing hide and seek, a car stopped. They kidnapped her. The children ran into the house trying to explain what had happened, but not a sound came out of their terrorized frozen throats. At nightfall, the people, frightened, rushed into their homes, shutting doors and windows. The village was silent.

Under a starry summer sky, a child's crying was heard in front of the house. "It's Sarah, sweet Sarah, sweet baby."

Once inside, little Sarah began talking, "I thought I was in a flying car. They put a scarf all around my face. I couldn't see. The men gave me candy and cookies. But someone stuck a needle in my arm. Look, just here." She showed her vein, smiled and said, "I'm so tired."

When the family gathered for breakfast the sun was almost at its zenith. "It's late. Is Sarah still sleeping?"

"She must be", said the mother. "I'll go get her." But she came back alone, livid, crying. "Sarah, poor Sarah, she's gone."

"But where? What do you mean?"

"Don't get excited, but listen to me, kids. Sarah is no longer with us. She died."

I wasn't there when it happened. But the story was told many times by the children, the parents, the people in the village. I cried and cursed, "I hate the Germans."

Poor Sarah, little sister, do you remember my funny evening song?

Yellow chick with silver wings,
Gentle flower dressed in red,
Sweet, it's time to go to bed

Each time I tell this story I feel my tears softly streaming down my cheeks. Sarah, my sister and Vincent, my son, the greatest losses I have experienced. The pain can't die but only be reborn.

Silence

There is no silence outside of you
There will always be a bird's wings flapping
A branch cracking
A stone falling down
A soft surge of water
There is no silence
But the silence of transcendency
Less than a second.

45

{ *White Linens and Nursery Rhymes* }

I got married on October 12, 1948 in the ancient church of St. Victor, known for its great bell with a resonant and deep voice. In Marseille, October is always glorious, sunny and crisp. That day was especially magnificent. The buses, cabs, street cars, and trains were all on strike, and so we walked through town from city hall to church and from church to home.

The wedding ceremony was simple but very beautiful. The church was filled with friends and one who was an organist played the music we wanted; Bach, Louis Milan, Marcel Dupre.

I didn't want to wear a wedding gown. I thought it was silly. My outfit was very elegant, a white skirt, six inches below the knees, a white blouse delicately embroidered by Lilly, my wonderful sister-in-law, a silk white hat with three white roses and one orange blossom, and white shoes, of course.

A few people were invited to dinner. It was still rationing time. Friendliness and simplicity, the whole thing was pleasant. But I didn't feel moved by it. I smiled gently with a sleepy heart.

The honeymoon voyage had to be canceled. The city was jammed with merchants, students, and tourists coming for the annual carnival. We finally found a small hotel in the lowest part of the town, Hotel de la Conception. What a trip.

We decided to live in Belgium. In Brussels, my husband's home town, the job search was more difficult than we had thought. My husband, Adrian, had just finished his Masters in Classical Studies; Greek, Latin, and history. With my degrees in psychology and modern literature, could I do better? I wasn't really sure.

So I decided to study journalism at the university, but just before the end of the school year I was sick. My first child was on her way. "Get an abortion. You won't be able to raise a baby", said my mother-in-law. I stood up for my choice and fought against the Flemish family tribe.

"My child is going to be born."

And she was born, on the same day my first poetry book was published. I was weak but I smiled to the visitors because baby Anne was so beautiful. Holding the infant close to my heart, I thought, "This child doesn't belong to me. She's not a piece of property. I'm here to love her, guide her, and help her grow on her own. That is what motherhood is for me."

Was I real? Did I want to be a perfect mother or did I want to be myself? My writing, at that time, expressed my ambivalence.

Trois Fleures

I found three flowers of China,
Do you want them? Here they are.
I found three flowers of China,
But don't pick them, oh please don't.

The first one has no thorn,
Do you want it? Here it is.
The first one has no thorn,
Just like a dispassionate heart.

The second one is white and fragile,
Do you want it? Here it is.

The second one is white and fragile,
But no one should gather it.

The third one is a bleeding flower,
Do you want it? Here it is.
The second one is a fragile flower,
Is a flower from which you die.

...I wondered if Paul Eluard would still like my poems.

There was Anne, my little Nanu, a little bird in the heart of a golden autumn; then came Vincent, so quiet, so fair, a little snow man born in the fire of July; then Sophie, Miss Never-Sleeps. They were sweet. They were fun. My love and my joy; mist and sunshine. Motherhood, a hint of release during those dormant years.

We moved to Liege where my husband got a very good job in an elitist school. We didn't want to leave the very sophisticated Brussels, afraid to live in a small town. But Liege is a very graceful place lounging between two dreamy rivers. People smile, stroll on bridges, stop at ice cream or chestnut stands according to the season, and talk to each other.

I found myself a part time job in a therapy center for families sponsored by the Rotary Club, the worst job of my entire life. It wasn't so easy with a thirteen month old baby and two small kids. I managed well. But how?

My husband was a good father. He could talk to the kids and play with them, but he never did much around the house. He spent most of the time in his studies. He didn't know anyone in Liege. His friends were the old friends from university years, but time had separated them. Adrian was very bright, speaking of ideas, philosophical concepts, intellectual books, but emotionally he wasn't there.

The chores were for me to do. Twice a week I had Yvonne. I found her through an acquaintance and she stayed with us for 16 years. When I met her I knew my search for help was over. Small, joyful, soft spoken, but strong. An iron hand in a velvet glove, I could trust her with the kids. Our friendship developed through the years and she became both my big sister and guardian angel.

For me there was never enough space to read and write. I was too busy with the children. I made three women friends in the neighborhood and we began to do things together with the children; walks, picnics, swims. Growing up the kids did a lot of sports; kayaking and swimming in summer and ice skating in winter. We gave each other support when something more difficult occurred.

The environment in Liege was quite good. Most of the kids in the neighborhood knew each other. Unfortunately, many of them had family problems. Their parents, to get rid of the kids, used to send them outside until late in the evening or give them plenty of money to see four or five movies throughout the weekend. On rainy Sunday afternoons, we opened our house to the neighborhood kids having talent shows, playing games, making projects, cooking crepes.

One Sunday afternoon a friend came to visit. The children were playing hide and seek. He was baffled. From under the table sprang an Asian girl. From behind the door appeared a little black boy from Zaire. In the middle of the room, talking and gesturing, was Sahid, a little boy from Morocco, as brown as a prune.

"Is this the United Nations?" my friend asked.

I laughed, "I wish the United Nations was as much fun as this."

For ten years I didn't publish anything. I hardly wrote, except once in a while here and there, a little story, a little poem. But it was something so rare. One morning I heard on the public radio that there was a poetry contest sponsored by the Society of Belgian Writers. The prize was 7,000 francs and publication of the book. I began to rummage through all the drawers of the house. My writings were everywhere because I didn't have any space for myself.

They wanted 24 poems. Did I write 24 poems in the last ten years? I was determined. I found some, wrote some, and put them together in an envelope. I was going to Brussels to visit Denise, my sister-in-law and planned to post them at the train station. But I got on the train and forgot. I approached a woman getting off the same train.

"Please, would you mind mailing this envelope? I will give you some money for the postage." She accepted, but I never knew if she mailed it. After all these years I still don't understand why I gave the envelope to a stranger. Was I trying to sabotage myself? Where was I and who was I at that time?

I waited and waited for three months. Then one day a telegram arrived: "First Prize from the Society of Belgian Writers".

In the beginning Adrian was delighted. "Bravo, Madame le Poet. I have something to be proud of, especially where I teach." But as I began being invited to read my poetry in literary clubs and started to go to Brussels very often, my husband began to dislike it.

"Do you think it is appropriate going to Brussels two or three times a week giving your lectures and leaving the children with the baby sitter? You have chosen to be a mother. Don't forget, the children need you here."

I argued. "I spend more time with the children than you do. I pay the baby sitter with the money I earn."

"That's not what I mean."

I understood exactly what he meant; to give up. And I did give up.

My growing little ones were dear to me, the most important part of my life. My creative energy became entirely oriented towards the children's welfare. Together we were dancing, singing, reading, cooking, baking pies, making perfumes and magical decoctions with flowers and herbs. With them I became a decorator, a storyteller, a playwright.

They taught me their games, their songs, their music. In exchange I was cuddling, nurturing, reassuring, easing the fever, washing the wound, nursing their hearts in pain, sharing their enthusiasm, empathizing with their disappointments, broken friendships, miscommunication with teachers. I was there for them. But where was I for myself? I stopped all the activities that would have pleased me. My health deteriorated. I had very low blood pressure. I got bronchitis, hemorrhages, and I almost died of salmonella.

At the university hospital I lay totally unconscious and was in a coma for five days. How did I come back?

Through the deep silence I heard a sound, faint but continuous, then the sound became clearly perceptible. I recognized the voice of an alto saxophone. The sound was increasing, approaching, and then filling my room playing a bluesy melody. Oh god, it was brilliant like a white light from another world. How long did the music last? I fell asleep peacefully.

In the morning when the nurse came my eyes were wide open. She touched my forehead. "Hello. Your fever is almost gone.'

"Was I really ill?"

"Well, you almost passed away. You were five days in a deep

coma, but this morning you look very much alive."

I told her my story and she laughed. She was a little nervous, I thought. "Oh", she said, "yes, we have so many cafes and bars around here, some students play music all night. I'm sure you heard some sort of saxophone.'

I smiled, "Oh, that's what it is."

While I was recovering in the hospital a friend who had stayed with the kids said they had been terrible the whole time. What could I say?

When I came home I felt very weak. I recovered slowly and began to play with the kids again. But I felt estranged from myself, protected, jailed, and cut off.

{ *Awareness* }

My husband, Adrian, became infatuated with one of his former students. She visited us often, playing guitar and singing with us. "I'm attracted to Helene," he said. "You'd better defend your kingdom."

"Are you the kingdom? Do you want me to fight Helene, to throw her out of the house? This is not my problem."

One day she called me, "Could we meet at the Esplanade cafe at 4:00?" When I arrived she was drinking a beer. "I really want to talk to you. You know, your husband asked me to be his lover."

"Why are you telling me this?"

"I want to be your friend and I'm afraid he will say things about me that aren't true. I am not his lover and I never will be." Instead, she and I became friends.

Early one morning after the children had just left for school, the telephone rang. It was my friend Mila's brother. "Nicolas, where are you?"

"I'm in Brussels, still acting at the Josephat Theatre. I thought you were in Brussels, too."

"What do you mean?'

"Well, I saw Adrian coming from the hotel across the street with a woman with your color hair. But I wasn't sure."

"Oh, Nicolas, why are you doing this," I said, but in my heart I suspected something. Adrian had been going to Brussels much too often.

"I don't know," he said. "I am beside myself. I guess I idolize this man too much. I'm sorry."

"Don't be sorry Nicolas, but I don't feel like talking anymore. Good-bye."

Throughout the day I worked with the telephone call in the back of my mind. When Adrian came home I asked, "How was Brussels?"

"It was okay. I spent the night at my sister's as usual."

Liar. I was disgusted. I wished I had a room for myself and said, "From now on I am going to sleep on the couch. You know that I need a lot of rest." I thought, one small room. Yes, Virginia Woolf, I am going to work my way out of here.

For some time I had an interest in alternative therapies and I thought that I should go back to school. I called the Institute of Psychology and they told me that they were starting a training at their new Carl Rogers Psychology Center. I signed up.

Adrian began to spend most of his weekends in Brussels. At Christmas time the kids helped me to fix the Christmas dinner and decorate the tree. Their father came home late. They were upset. Later I asked him, "Why are you doing this to the children?"

"I don't know. I'm obsessed with a woman, but I love you."

"I don't love you. And today, at this very minute I realize that I never did." Feelings and questions began to rush through my mind. Why had I married this man? Why? In the three years of betrothal I had broken my engagement three times.

A few months before I had rented a studio for sculpting in a hippie community. It was a big room with no water and I furnished it with a table and four chairs and a little stove in order to be able to make some tea or coffee in the winter.

On Wednesday afternoons my daughter Sophie and I had been spending time there. She was thirteen years old. We played with clay

54

or paper maché and then she would go home. I would stay to finish my sculptures and the hours sped by as I worked. Sometimes I spent the night there. I loved it there.

To make myself more comfortable I bought a rubber pad, some sheets and blankets, and a gas heater on wheels. The studio was quiet. As time passed I stayed there more and more, and quite suddenly, I decided to move in.

Sophie, her friend Cecile, and I made curtains out of a burlap sack that we embroidered with multicolored thread. I was so proud of my two small windows. I bought an old wardrobe at the flea market and made a big curtain to separate a small kitchen area.

I was alone with no money, not even running water in my room. Every morning I went down the hall to fill my kettle, warming the water and washing myself in a big bucket, just the way the ancients did.

Happiness began to creep into my heart. I had left comfort and security to undertake a new journey.

{ *The House By The Swamp* }

We were twelve living in the house. The neighbors named the place "The Gentle Hippies' Home" although the '60s had already faded away. The community activities were varied. We managed a bookstore. We did poetry readings one evening a week. We participated in street fairs and neighborhood festivities.

Many artists, friends, musicians, painters and writers haunted the house like benevolent spirits. But Jean Paul's writings were the most remarkable. Mila introduced me to him after one of these literary evenings. All night we read and talked.

He told me about his wife, yet another Helene. "Yes, she had an accident when she was a child. They had to amputate two fingers on her left hand and she still can't accept it. She's always hiding her hand under a shawl and never uses it in front of people. She is a social worker in the little town of Vervieres. I teach ethics and some first notions of philosophy in the public school in that same town."

As time passed Jean Paul and I became good friends. I admired his work and he admired mine. One Friday afternoon as I was just finishing a children's story, Jean Paul paid me a visit. "Helene is downstairs and I would like you to meet her. Can she come up?"

"Of course she can."

"Come on in, Helene. This is Josée, a great writer."

"Hi, Helene."

"Oh, hi. My husband read some of your stories to me so I feel as if I already know you.'

"Also, if you are free this weekend we would like to invite you to our home. We live quite alone by the forest not far from the swamp.

56

We hear only frogs, birds, and some wild game at night."

"Well, I don't have any plans."

Her voice struck me as polished, controlled, cool, or I thought, perhaps cruel. Am I going to be prejudiced because of her voice?

"We'll pick you up tomorrow around 4:00 p.m.," said Jean Paul.

On Saturday Jean Paul came alone. "Before going home we are going to say hello to one of my friends. He is from Africa and just graduated from school yesterday. He's a lawyer now."

We arrived at Henri's studio. "Congratulations, Henri." His studio was small but for a few minutes I believed that Henri was a giant.

"We're having dinner at home. Why don't you join us?" asked Jean Paul.

"No. I need to rest. I want to be by myself."

"All right, buddy. Good bye." Jean Paul took my arm. "Let's go get Helene. We have to cook."

In the car Helene asked me if I had some money. "I forgot my wallet and I have to do some shopping. I will give you the money back tonight."

Their place seemed like magic. An early spring twilight was already waking up the creatures of the night. An enormous dog barked. "It's our Doberman, Marco." I shivered. A Doberman, my god. In a flash of images I saw a watch tower, a patrol of SS, a train jammed with prisoners disappearing into the fog. Am I still traumatized? Can't I forget? What does Marco have to do with the German occupation? Am I crazy? It's so nice here.

"Women, come inside and sit down. Listen. I have a Freemason lodge meeting. It's 7:00 p.m. now. At 9:00 p.m. I'll be back and make the Chinese soup that I promised you. So don't stuff yourselves."

We laughed. "Au revoir."

Helene began to talk about her job and how great it was to live in this house.

"I think Jean Paul told me that you have a little boy."

"Yes, he's at my mother's. We don't want to have him here when we have friends over. He gets bored." Then we heard a motor bike. She opened the door. "Oh, Henri is here. He changed his mind. Fine."

The giant stepped into the room. "Is there something to drink?"

"Not yet. I thought of going to the village."

"I'll go".

Henri came back with a big bottle of juniper liquor. "It's a specialty of Belgium and Holland. It's a hard, transparent drink enclosed in a beautiful ceramic container." Henri and Helene began to drink avidly. I hesitated. Finally I took a small glass.

"Is that all you want?"

"Well, I'm not used to drinking these kind of things. I like it in small doses. It tastes bizarre," I said, "just like ether. Don't you think so?"

They laughed. "Not at all. It's your imagination. Maybe you haven't drunk liquor for a while."

"That's true. Maybe I don't remember the flavor".

We kept on talking and joking, but I felt wary. I thought it was already long past 9:00 p.m. I had a strange sensation that my head was spinning. The voices became murmurs. The giant got up and walked behind me, touched the back of my head at two pressure points close to the ears and I passed out.

Was I dreaming a nightmare? I was fighting a giant and the dog, throwing dishes on the floor, kicking down tables, breaking chairs. There was a cigarette smell, a thick smoke, and my body punctured with burning spots.

In the morning I woke up in the little boy's bedroom with a heavy wooden board lying on top of me. "Oh," said Helene, "the board of his electric train fell off the shelf. Did you feel it? Did you get hurt?"

"No, I didn't feel it." I got up and came down to the living room. It was a mess. Everything was on the ground and it smelled of alcohol, food, and cigarettes. I was angry. "I'm going to take a bath and then you will drive me home immediately."

They drove me home and left and I called a friend of mine who was a nurse.. I told her my story and asked her to come right away.

"My god", she said, "you have cigarette burns all over your body."

"Yes. My head hurts. I'm very sick." Mila also came over and for three days they nursed me.

"Mila, how well do you know Jean Paul?"

"Yes, I should have told you, but I never thought he would invite you there. I never thought they would. He did that to me and even worse. I had to flee in the middle of the night. I ran three miles to the village inn. It was horrible. I was so frightened.'

"But Mila, you never told me.'

"I was so ashamed."

"I am not. I'm going to tell everyone in the community and all around." And I did. There was no more room for victimization.

Across the backyard from the community house was a little cottage that Jean Paul wanted to rent. He had made a deal with Richard, the actor, a member of our community who lived next door with his wife and little boy. "I want to write peacefully and be by myself," Jean Paul had said. But when he came to pay the first month rent the people of the house confronted him angrily, "Go away. You had better never set foot in this house, this neighborhood, or on this street. You had better watch out."

Several women came up with similar frightening stories and an article was written in the local newspaper. Jean Paul was fired from the school and Helene also lost her job. They left the region and we never heard from them again. Where did they go to perpetrate their criminal rites?

Is this story the repetition of my sixth birthday? Was I repeating a lesson that I hadn't learned? When I had been victimized as a child I closed up and didn't talk to anyone about my experience. I must have been so ashamed by what had happened to me that I never shared my experience until a few years ago. This time I stood my ground.

{ *The Puma* }

A few years later living in Brussels, I realized that I had finally learned my painful lesson. Sometimes on Saturday nights I would go dancing with three other girlfriends. Our favorite club was The Puma. To get in we had to be introduced by two people named godparents. We had to pay a membership fee and present our club card each time. We could drink fruit juices and soft beverages without being perceived as phonies.

One Saturday evening a man introduced himself to Adriana and started a conversation. She returned to our table. "He wants to invite me to a party", she said.

"Are you going?"

"No. I'm staying with you. I don't go to parties with strangers."

The man came to our table with beer. "I see that you are a group of friends, so I invite you all. The party is at the home of my closest friends and you will meet plenty of nice people."

"In this case we'll go."

"Yes, let's go."

I wasn't very enthusiastic, but I followed the other women. It wasn't very far from the club. We came into a vast apartment, practically empty,- just a couch in the middle of the room, a counter covered with glasses and bottles, and a steep stairway leading to a loft.

Suddenly a naked man came down shouting, 'hooray, hooray", jumping and hopping. His body was full of tattoos. He grabbed Adriana, "Come and dance." But we all got up. "We do everything together. This is a family". Then we sat down and the man seemed displeased. A bartender came over to us, 'A drink, a little vodka?"

"No, we don't drink."

"Just a taste", he said, and poured four small glasses.

I took one and carefully smelled it. "Don't drink", I whispered. "Let's get out of here right away." We grabbed our coats as fast as we could and ran quickly down stairs.

The guys yelled after us, "Hey, you. Stay here. Don't leave." Then they started hurling insults, calling us names. We crammed into Claire's minicar and left. The men reaching the street too late to stop us.

"Was there a chemical in the vodka? How did you know?"

"Well, I learned through the teachings of life. Did you ever read a better book?"

{ *The Statue* }

I remember my little statue, probably one of my best pieces. It was a small woman in green carrying a bundle of wood, a *fagot* in French. She was an old country person who had an air of resignation. These verses of a song had inspired me:

There was once an old woman. She was looking for wood in the forest to warm her man's body for he was dying a natural death. She was tired and very cold because it was winter. Sometimes in her heart she would hear a mocking voice: 'Remember how unfaithful he was'. But the man was dying. So she was carrying her bundle of wood to make a fire to warm up her man who was dying a natural death.

My little statue was in our community bookstore sitting in the window. Many people stopped to look at her. But one day someone came into the store and bought it.

A few months later, the city politicians decided to cut down the trees in our neighborhood square. Plain trees and linden trees, old and beautiful, in order to make a rink for ice skating and a big gymnasium. Immediately the gentle hippies gave the alert, mobilized the neighborhood. Diligently we went from house to house with letters and petitions. Arlette and I spotted a small cottage. A woman opened the door and said, "Come in, come in. You must be tired. Have you been walking all day?"

"More or less", we smiled.

"Oh, your green statue", Arlette said.

"Yes, I bought it in Roture in the bookstore."

"Oh, but it's my statue..."

"What do you mean?"

" ..my piece."

"Oh", she exclaimed, "You are the artist?" She smiled and hugged me. "This reminds me of the song The Woman With Her Fagot."

"That's what inspired me."

"Oh, I really love her. She brings back so many memories. I'm Jacqueline," she said and signed our petition. So all together we saved the trees.

{ *Catharsis* }

I went to visit some friends who were living in a community in the country. It was a glorious October day and I was enjoying people and the mood of autumn. We cooked all day and set a big round table. Mary-France smiled, "We are waiting for plenty of new guests today, but my god, you made chocolate mousse for an army."

"But I don't have any sense of proportions, you know that."

She dipped her fingers in my preparation. "Mmmm. It's firm, creamy, and tasty."

When the guests arrived we sat around the table and the man on the left introduced himself, "I'm Federico from Bari, Italy, but they call me Rico." His soft voice with the strong Italian accent brought back images of early childhood. I saw a little girl climbing a steep ladder, bringing food to the old Italian man living in the attic. The international police were searching for him. He had been a famous engineer in Italy. They said he had already invented a car that didn't need oil.

Rico and I talked about many things. He praised my dessert and invited me for a walk in the orchards. Apples and pears moistened the ground and exhaled a perfume of fermented wine.

Later, Rico came to Liege to visit my studio. I began to see him in Brussels almost every weekend. He talked about his childhood in Italy and his admiration for Mussolini. As a young spy during the war he had been caught and tortured by American soldiers, condemned to death, but acquitted because of his age.

I asked many questions but I restrained myself from judging. I thought of Nina. He was a very literate and bright man and we read Nietzsche and Ungaritti. He was also a marvelous cook with an eclectic personality. We became lovers, experiencing a sensuous, sophisticated and passionate relationship.

Reflection

Your companionship is fire
Burning without combustion

Rico was an angry man and after a while I suspected that he was an alcoholic. I didn't want to face it, but a year later I couldn't deny it. He was drinking hard liquor and we fought violently. It was difficult and painful. At times we went out all night and slept all day. Often, he would leave me alone in a cafe and run around with other women, buying them roses. One day, sick at heart I decided not to wait for him. I took a cab home.

At home the telephone began to ring, for hours and hours, but I didn't answer. Rico came by, knocking at the door. I still didn't answer. But he began to bang loudly and I opened the door slightly. "What do you want?"

"I looked for you all over town. I was worried about you." He started to shout and call me names and tried to push the door in. But I was strong and closed it.

"I don't want to see you. This time I don't need to fight or go to your place and break everything again. I don't want anything to do with a bum of your kind. Good-bye." Did I reach my limit suddenly? All my feelings for this man were gone. I felt relieved and purified.

It was during this tumultuous period that I was browsing among the new therapies. I had moved to Brussels several months before, determined to find a better place to live, a richer environment, and more opportunities for studying.

Also my handmade jewelry was picking up fast. People liked my original creative work. I was good at making money and could afford to go to different workshops: transactional analysis, neuro-linguistic programming (NLP), mental dynamics, reflexology and massage. I was a dilettante in therapies like other people are in music or literature. What was I seeking?

I stepped into Gestalt therapy. "You are a magnet," said Denys, my teacher, "it is a gift, a responsibility, too. Can't you stick to something seriously? Can't you choose?"

I decided to do my training with him. I was thrilled with my work and didn't rebel against the technical part. My imaginative nature was excited by using day dreams, movements, situations, expressions. He was assisting me, or rather, supervising my work. He didn't talk much during my first group experience even though I was sweating, my face as gray as paper mache. When the people left I was shaking and crying. Denys asked, "What is going on? I think you did an excellent job. Do you want to talk about it for a while?"

I moved into a bigger apartment with a separate room for my

clients. I loved my work. A few months later I heard about a psychologist who was looking for an assistant in Reikian bio-energy and was willing to provide training. I applied, was interviewed, got the job, and signed a two year contract. We planned to do two weekend workshops every month and some marathon four to five day workshops a few times a year. Antoine was a former Dominican priest. He had studied philosophy, theology, psychology, and then chose to become a therapist.

When I first met him, he said, "I know you."

"Yes, you seem familiar to me also."

"Oh, I saw you at the Psychological Institute in Liege." I thought it would be fun working with someone who wasn't a total stranger.

A little bit shy, I arrived one Saturday morning at André's to teach and co-facilitate my first weekend workshop. A few people who had come the night before from different towns were having breakfast in the kitchen. I mingled, talked, and had coffee.

The house was big, with several bedrooms, two huge rooms transformed into dormitories, and a few little spaces with couches and folding beds. All these people were going to be together for the weekend. That was the rule, whether we did long or short workshops. The working space was vast, clean, plenty of pillows on the floor and a mattress in the middle, as was common in many therapy centers at the time.

There was also an orgone box in the hall. They were very popular during the 60's and 70's. They were large boxes made up of layers of metal, wood, and cotton that you sat inside on a stool. They had been invented by Wilhelm Reich in order to feel, see, and capture cosmic sexual energy. I felt a surge of hot energy when I went inside. It was fun.

Just before the workshop started, Antoine took me aside.

"I want the participants to be naked."

"What is the point?"

"They don't need to be in disguise. They don't have to hide themselves behind nice clothes. I want to break through appearances. Are you okay with that?"

"I'm okay. But what difference does it make? Me, I won't see them. But they will compare their bodies with each other, their scars, their stretch marks, their fat." But we did it anyway.

The group started. We used a mixture of bio-energy, Gestalt, bodywork, psychodrama, rebirthing, and chaos, or maybe synthesis. When we weren't naked, Antoine wore a long yellow robe with his long blond hair and his shaved round face. He really looked like an archangel,- calm, poised, majestic. The guru, I thought, the master well played.

For the first several months I worked well with the people and they were opening up emotionally. They were trusting. Antoine was pleased too, at first, but then I felt a kind of exasperation from him. Before my first marathon he told me, "You have changed the spirit of my work. I want people to have free sex and to love anyone unconditionally. The human body is completely lovable."

"Yes, I agree. But I don't want free sex as part of my group," I said. "I don't use people to satisfy my own needs. But tomorrow is the marathon and people have paid. It has to be done."

I had been witnessing, with discontentment, the high priest of love working in his temple, using men and women to fulfill his fantasies. During the marathon weekend I heard rumors and complaints among the participants. Then came the rebellion and half the group refused to work with him. "I'm sorry, but we can't work together. Go downstairs, I'll stay here. They can choose to work with only one of us." We had two more days to go.

At the end of the second day, my group was in a circle. We decided to share some experiences, do a deep relaxation, and take some time to say a friendly good-bye. Unexpectedly, Antoine barged in the room. He waited for a while and then said, "Aha! What have you done to them? Did you give them some valium?"

"No, why?"

"My clients upstairs are so excited."

"Well, maybe we have different ways of working with people." That day I ended my contract.

{ The Gamelan }

My practice was growing. For a long time, Martine, Suzanne, Anne-Marie and I wanted to work together. We decided to open up a healing center with all kinds of therapy; natural dance, bio-energy, massage, rebirth, bodywork, musical therapy, and more. Where were we going to find a house big enough in Brussels to contain all our dreams?

But we found it. A three-story house with a cement backyard in a quiet little street, although it was in a very lively part of town. The house may have been built in the 20's but it had been badly kept and partially abandoned. Cheap rent and a lot of space, exactly what we needed, except that the place was almost in ruins. "It's going to be a lot of work," I thought.

We replaced the water pipes, gas pipes, the electricity. We tore down walls to enlarge some rooms, painted it, cleaned the attic and transformed it into a workshop. The landlord agreed to everything verbally and promised us that we could pay only half the rent for three years. We named the house Gamelan.

We opened up the center with a staff of seven people. We organized programs, files, mailing lists. It is rare to see so many creative people working together. We reserved some evenings for neighborhood contact; exchanging furniture, clothes, books, records. We developed trust and friendship and a sense of community. We changed the energy of the old place and soon the Gamelan became a big success.

There was room for self expression, imagination, group experimentation, movement, music, contact. It was a space of all possibilities. Energetic, enthusiastic, and confident, we had a goal, helping people find their own path, following them through their transformations if they wanted, helping them to be who they could be. There were no priests, no gurus, no masters, only mentors and companions.

Did the fool leap too high or fall or dive into the muddy ocean of the devil?

{ *Adventure In Shadows* }

In August 1980, my friend Andrée offered me a trip to California. "My father died and left me some money. I don't want to go alone. I like your company. All you have to do is to pay for your own food."

Going to America! When I was five my father punished me for something I don't remember. He had never punished me before and I was shocked. So I went into my little room, got a small bag, packed a pair of socks, a little panty, a dress and a handkerchief, and left. I waited for the streetcar in the rain. When it arrived, I got on and sat down in the back. The driver called out, "Miss, miss, your money."

"I don't have any money."

"Where are you going?"

"I'm going to America." At the next stop he made me get off. "Now I have to find my way home," I thought. I wandered along the damp streets for a long time. Then I ran into Spartico, my older brother's friend, who brought me home. Whenever the kids teased me and didn't want to play with me I thought, "I am going to go to America. There I will find plenty of good people and children to play with me." Well, I finally was getting the chance.

We flew to California. From the airport we went to Berkeley. It was Andrée's idea. She spoke English pretty poorly, but people could understand her. I didn't speak any at all. We took long walks from the Marina to the campus of the University and along Shattuck and Telegraph Avenues. We found workshops to do, dirty motels, and a holistic center. Bruce, the manager of the center told my friend, "My sister lives in San Francisco. Every summer she rents a room to visitors, but I don't think she has anybody this year."

Andrée said it would be interesting to live with an American family. So Bruce called his sister and in the evening we arrived in Noe Valley at Lane and Pat's flat. The following morning we went from bookstores to herb shops to the Star Magic Store to Real Food, walking through the streets. I heard her voice and I met her soul - San Francisco.

{ *Fascination* }

What is it? A connection? A special vibration? Many cities are beautiful with parks, fountains, little cafes. Are people different in San Francisco? Is there a kind of awareness in the trees, in the grass, in the stone, in the wood? We visited beautiful places; Monterey, Carmel, Esalen with its old shops, its hot tubs, and the cliffs plunging into the ocean. We drove around the wine country. We visited other places but I was always longing for San Francisco. "Let's go back."

For three weeks we didn't leave the city. My fascination was contagious. Back on the plane I cried, "in a year I will be here. This place is going to be my hometown." How can I describe my experience? I can't find any words. For the very first time in my life I had a sense of belonging. My nomadic spirit had found its oasis.

My partners were distressed when I told them my decision to move. How long could I stay? Could I so quickly give up my responsibilities? What if I had been mistaken by my imagination? And what if the whole thing were only infatuation? "I have to go. I have to be there to fulfill my destiny."

A few friends took me to the airport one morning in August 1981. Flight delayed. Departure 3:00 p.m. We went back home and had lunch and then back to the airport. The plane was delayed again. We walked around, went for coffee, and then found a dying bird. Hildegarde took some of her rescue remedies from her purse and opened its beak. The liquid went down the bird's throat. We waited and waited. After fifteen minutes the bird stirred and then spread its wings and flew into the sky. Was it a good omen?

The air traffic controllers were on strike, the first big strike of the Reagan years. We landed in New York at three in the morning and I called a friend in New York who had been expecting me. Henri was sleeping.

"I went three times to pick you up at the airport. They couldn't tell me when the plane would arrive."

"It's okay. I'll take a cab."

"Do you think you can?"

"Give me all the directions and the address." I listened carefully to his pronunciation, but fortunately the cab driver was from Haiti and spoke French! It was hot in New York. I spent ten days in a steamy town but I loved it.

My budget was very limited. To spare money I took a Trailways bus from New York to San Francisco. Four days and three nights in the dust and heat, sweating, eating junk food, speaking no English. A young man sat beside me and said a few words, but gave up. Finally, I answered him in French, *"Comprends pas."* He was from Baton Rouge, was a French teacher, and was going to Oakland. Synchronicity, my great protector in life, had found me again and I had found a companion for my long journey. In Oakland, at my stop I asked, "Are we going to see each other again?"

"I am visiting a friend for a few days," he said. "We are just like the birds. Maybe sometime we might meet in a train station, in a cafe, somewhere in a strange town or never."

My arrival in San Francisco was rather dramatic. From New York, Henri had called his friend Sam to come and get me at the bus terminal. I showed him a piece of paper with three addresses, but none of these places existed anymore. I was worried. He tried to talk to me but I couldn't understand. The only thing I could hear was "okay, okay". At last he stopped his car in front of a house and we went in. He said a few words to a woman and she spoke to me. *"Bonsoir madame."* To my surprise she was French.

76

Princess of Compassion - acrylic on canvas, 1992

Confetti Heart - acrylic on canvas, 1990

Night Cries - acrylic on canvas, 1999

Coyote Messenger - acrylic on canvas, 1995

{ *Horsetail Hotel* }

There I was - haggard, dizzy, dirty, smelly, carrying a big suitcase with my belongings for how many months? Mrs. Faubert, the keeper of the French Residence Club, showed me around and led me to my room. The only thing I noticed was the elevator, a real monument. How can I describe it? Imagine a small cage with two metallic doors attached that seemed to be made of metal bars like a fence or a prison. I was hungry but the evening meal was over and I didn't know the neighborhood. So I went to bed and slept for two days.

In The Morning

In the morning people get up
Shedding their dreams
In order to be ready for the day
They want to look at the sky
But their eyelids are drooping
Still heavy from their night journey
How is the weather today?
Is it the wind of change
Blowing the leaves down to the ground?

At breakfast I sat at a table by myself. A waitress with a beautiful voice asked me, "What would you like to eat?" I heard a light accent.

"Oh, you speak French."

"Yes, I lived in Paris but I am from England. My name is Olivia. Would you like to go for a walk today?" We wandered around North Beach and talked, slowly opening the door to a friendship, unfolding through the years as a richly colored garland of love and still alive today.

I became acquainted with the nature of the Residence Club's tenants. Some stopped there for a while, some for a few years, and some probably forever. There were students finishing summer school, Italian ones, wild and noisy, French, Japanese, Brazilian, polite and serious. There were some businessmen passing by as quick as shooting stars. There were other people who seemed to live there forever, fearful, depressed, cut off from the world. The owner's family was uptight, narrow minded, controlling and pretentious - a caricature of the French culture. Even the dog, Coco, was unattractive and nasty.

I discovered San Francisco's neighborhoods; Union Square, where I spent a lot of time reading and listening, Chinatown, North Beach, sitting in Washington Square and hearing people speak Chinese or Italian. The Italian language brought back memories; the exuberance of Naples and Calabria in spring with a scent of jasmine and bergamotte. Was San Francisco already present in my past?

Impressions, moods, hills, people, and the cafe. It felt like Marseilles, Naples, all the Mediterranean coast, and also the primitive Abruzzi. I recalled the crisp summer evenings of Jerusalem, the beaches of Allecante, the mysterious Andalusia. I recalled that which is white and is delicate as the flower, as the flower contains the microcosm of the planet. No need to travel anymore. The entire world is here in San Francisco.

Olivia moved from the Residence Club first. She became a boat sitter. My first visit to the ship was quite an adventure. "You can't come onto the pier without a key. Wait for me at the gate." We walked along the bay for a while, reached a boat and jumped in.

"Is it moving like this all the time?"

"Yes, I am used to the gentle rocking." She had prepared an enormous seasonal salad. As broke as we were, we always managed to eat well. "Let me go get my laundry", she said. But when she returned with her clothes, she fell into the bay. "Help me, help me," she cried.

I was in a big panic but I inched cautiously towards their edge of the boat. I was scared of the water. What if I fell into the bay, too? We would both drown. I don't know what happened but somehow she propped herself over the railing.

"I had better go take a shower now." She left the boat again but this time came back safely. We laughed and are still laughing when we talk about it.

{ *Apprenticeship* }

A few weeks after my arrival, I was referred to the Lighthouse for the Blind, where I learned English and found interesting things to do. However, since my brief stay at the boarding school, I had never lived with so many blind people. There, the kids had been my playmates, and together we went through serious training for life. Here, there were mostly elderly people who had lost their sight recently and were simply trying to adjust. A shower of sad feelings fell upon my heart. I felt naturally attracted to the staff persons even though they were sighted since I could relate to them not as a blind client, but as myself.

One of them, Sue, tried to talk to me desperately. When I asked her later why she tried so hard she said, "You seemed so bright, attractive, and interesting. I was fascinated. I wondered why you were here."

"Sometimes we are fascinated by people we don't understand. I guess we project onto them our own image," I replied.

I attended my first English class and met Norma, one of my blessings. I realized that being an avid student was part of me and would be until I died. I also moved from the Residence Club. Sue helped me find a room in a Victorian house on Oak Street. The man living there was an episodic client at the Lighthouse, the father of five kids, divorced, and living alone in his big home. The rent was cheap and I could use the living room and the kitchen. I had a good time there for a while.

Yves, one of my son's friends came to San Francisco and rented a room in the same house. We took endless walks in the morning that made us stiff. We cooked. We played music. We talked. It was party time.

Olivia invited Yves and me to spend Thanksgiving on a boat belonging to some friends of hers - our first Thanksgiving in America. Fruitcake breakfast and turkey dinner, new flavors; sweet potatoes, cranberry sauce, pumpkin pie. It didn't take me long to get used to new food, new tastes, new drinks. People were friendly and by now I could speak a little bit of English. It helped.

It was windy and rainy that day and the rough rocking of the boat made Yves sick. So sick that he turned from flesh colored to green. I don't think he will ever forget his first Thanksgiving in America.

Our landlord invited us everywhere; union parties, cafeteria parties, family reunions, New Year's meetings. I listened and learned as people asked me questions all the time and I tried to answer, to speak. I would come back to my bedroom with terrible headaches, but full of new idioms.

San Francisco, Mid summer night. Silence, but how many presences around The spirits' breath fills the quietness and I am aware of connections. I am not alone. I have guides and companions on all different planes. Maybe that's why I like to live by myself. The longing of the heart is human, but the flight of the soul takes you to the divine light. Unfortunately, it's not so easy to lift our heavy butts. We sit and cry for love and love is all around. We just don't know how to get it. Social myths, family myths, roles, functions, dogma, taboos. Give me a break. I want to breathe, to choose my family, my environment, and change my belief system when it no longer helps me ... or perhaps not have a belief system at all.

It was the end of January and an apocalyptic storm was hitting Brussels. My Belgian friends called, "It's important, the old landlord is taking us to court. You have to come back." When I arrived, I found the house damp with a vague odor of mildew. Marcel had tried to keep the vessel above water but it was almost impossible. The wind had torn down the chimney and destroyed part of the roof. Together, we struggled and fixed the house again. During all that spring, the Gamelan was renewed. "I will help you as much as I can," I said to my partners, "but my life is not here anymore. You are important to me. It hasn't been easy to leave my work behind, but I want to go back to San Francisco."

I returned to San Francisco on the first of July. The summer was exceptionally hot and the house was invaded by Belgian people whom I vaguely knew. They were libertines, nosy, and intrusive. I didn't enjoy the barbecues in the park with the landlord's family and the huge mixed cake dripping with multicolored artificial cream; the smell of roasted meat and greasy sauce; people shouting, playing games, drinking beer, wind and Coca-Cola; obnoxious kids smeared with ketchup gushing from their hamburgers; family gossip; TV soap operas; and small talk.

"You're lucky," said Olivia, "you are learning the American mainstream culture."

"Oh yes. What an experience. Now I know."

{ *Fear and Release* }

This morning I heard Marcel's voice on the telephone. "Hey in three weeks I will finish my NLP masters."

Congratulations, Master Marcel. I remember we called him the little green man, the Indian from the second floor. "So, what are you going to do now?"

"Well, I guess I'm going to help other people."

"I'm not surprised and I'm very happy. I feel like singing 'Oh, carry me back to old Gamelan where trust and friendship can grow'." I remember the people calling aloud, running down the stairs, talking and playing.

I made a few trips between Brussels and San Francisco. Finally, we abandoned the Gamelan. The landlord had taken us to court with an historical document. The house had been classified as a historical building and we never had the right to transform it. He had never mentioned that to us but we couldn't prove it. As the founder of the Gamelan, I felt responsible for the fines, and for eight years I paid for my mistake. It seems so long ago now.

I remember Guru, our black cat so wild and crazy. Only when Marcel was home was she soft and peaceful. She could hear him coming up the sidewalk even before he had opened the front door. How could she know? Maybe she was psychic? A real Guru! She was certainly psychosomething, like everybody else in the house anyway. Some clients were afraid of her. One day she got wilder, rushed in the street and got run over. And then, the Gamelan died. But for the people it wasn't death, it was change through transformation, new beginnings, spiritual unfolding. I recall those things but I don't feel any regret. I love the people who shared with me this unusual experience.

In 1984, I was asked to do a documentary for the French CBC (Canadian Broadcasting Company) in Vancouver. The man who interviewed me told me that I could stay with his family. "We have to do the job before the end of December, my wife is expecting our child before the end of January." Sion and Marcia were warm and open. We began to work intensely. I was delighted with the studio equipment, the echo machine, the work outside in cafes and movie houses. They introduced me to their friends.

"We have never had a Christmas Eve dinner. But this year Hanukkah ends the same day, so we can have one."

"And what if the baby arrives on Christmas Eve?"

"It's due the end of January."

"Hmm, I'm not so sure. My feeling is that you are going to have a little Jesus." Sure enough, on Christmas Eve a little Jewish boy, Adam Assouline, was born.

The job done, I was scheduled to leave. But at the airport, I was detained by American immigration for over a week. Apparently, I was on the verge of being deported though I had no idea why. Furthermore, it was holiday time and I didn't know where to turn.

While I was stuck in Vancouver, I tried to earn a little bit of money doing massage and psychic readings. Finally, I was received by the Belgian counsel and two days later I was given approval to return to the US with an apology from the INS, as well as a prolonged visa. Later, when my visa did expire I had the choice to go back to Belgium or become an illegal alien, and I was one for six years, confident that they wouldn't deport me. Fearless me, completely. Finally, I had released myself from bureaucracy.

{ Images and Reflections }

Lying down with a broken knee there is not much to do, so I decided to write this book, since this may be a time of rest, meditation and remembrances. But I don't mean "the good old days." I always laugh when I hear that expression. For me, each season has its good and bad days. When a page is turned, I have no regrets. I go on with the book of my life. Each breath, each one of my actions and reactions expresses my essence.

Plunging into the past is probably trying to capture the essential oil of my being; a mysterious part of me that I want to feel, to know, to understand better. I turn back some pages to look at scenes and pictures in order to comprehend their power in my present.

Impressions

A soothing river
Crossing a sunny plain
I hear an echo of Debussey
Reflections on the water

A bell ringing in my heart
Deep chords
Dark notes
Contrasts.

Blue icy blue
Pink and grey

A breeze colors my cheeks
Tosses my hair

I am lost in years
Is it the beginning or the end
Of our century?

A promenade where my life is still strolling
A dress creme and gold
A white hat with flowing feathers

Blue icy blue
Pink and grey

A woman walking around the wail of her melancholy
Lonely among the flowers of her dreams

Crystal beads
Pendant from her fragile neck
A corsage
A grand piano

Blue icy blue
Pink and grey.

Once Grandfather Philippe had a hunting dog that he loved very much. My brother and some other boys taught the dog to attack small farm animals; roosters, geese, ducks and even cats. Grandfather Philippe talked to them, "Each time the dog kills an animal, I have to pay. People are going to sue me if you keep doing it." But the boys enjoyed their cruel game. Grandfather Philippe spoke to the boys again. "What shall I do? Hit you? Lock you in the basement?" The boys didn't care. They must have been very proud of themselves. Sometimes they took the dog and attached all kinds of things around its tail; old shoes, old pots, cow bells, anything that could make noise. One afternoon they were teasing the dog mercilessly. Grandfather came with his rifle. "Now boys, line up behind me." He shot the dog. "She's gone now. Your cruelty can't reach her anymore."

Sometimes the image of my grandmother invades my imagination and I push it away. I am not Grandma, I am sweet and small. She chose to be a big ugly thing. Can I judge her? When I returned to Corsica I was twelve years old, already with the shaped body of a young woman. As if I am a child again, before me is Grandfather Philippe. I hear his voice, his words; he is so good to me.

I was told that Grandfather Philippe had killed a man who had courted his wife when she was young and attractive. Grandmother and the man would meet at the village fountain in the evening when she went to draw water. They would have long talks when they met and this would make Grandfather very jealous. He asked Grandmother to stop flirting with the man, but she wouldn't. So he killed the man and fled into the woods.

When World War One broke out he wasn't required to serve in the army since he already had seven children. But he surrendered himself to the police and asked to go into the army as a volunteer instead of going to prison. He was sent to Africa for five years and Grandmother raised her seven children alone.

When he came back they had ten more kids. What a life. Did she try to drown me, fearful that I would become as miserable as she was? I am sorry, Grandma. Whatever you have done to me, now I can forgive you.

I entered the classroom. "I would like to learn the Braille/English contraction system.' A kind woman put my hand on a chair.

"I am Dottie. Sit down. I would be pleased to teach you."

My English was still on the broken side. Sometimes she had to explain words. But the book she gave me to read was fun - a story about a German family coming to America interested in getting information about American schools, food, teenagers and adaptation to an American lifestyle. It was very instructive for me. While I was studying Braille contractions, I was also trying to smooth out my English.

Two months later it was over. I didn't want to leave the class. I went to the main teacher, Bill Barker, to ask if I could volunteer to teach Braille. To my surprise, he accepted me. In time I discovered that he was a great musician and I began to take singing lessons from him. I was really happy to get back to music. I learned also that he taught piano, so I decided to check what was left from my childhood. To my astonishment, I could read Braille music pretty accurately. Read with the left and play with the right, read with the right and play with the left, memorize a few bars at a time, then put it all together. I memorized a Scarlatti sonata.

One day he brought in the Bach Prelude, in C minor. "We are going to play it together for Christmas."

"In public?"

"Yes."

"Oh god, I can't believe it." We played it. He congratulated me, but I still think that it was a flop. My piano lessons with Bill didn't last very long.

Feelings from the past surge from my subconscious mind. I remember Mademoiselle Jeanne, my piano teacher when I was twelve.

Each time we made a mistake she would twist our hands or hit our fingertips with a ruler. Mendelson got me. I was spinning and spinning the piece, it was so difficult. She hit my fingers so many times that I quit.

Several years before that my father had wanted me to learn violin. I wanted to learn silver flute.

"Silver flute, that's not for a woman. In Greece, only courtesans play the silver flute," he said.

"Who were they? I don't care about Greece."

For Christmas I asked for a train. By the chimney there was a huge cardboard box with a bow. "Oh, my train!", I cried. Excited, I opened it up as fast as I could. There was a beautiful wooden case and inside a violin. I refused to take lessons, but all day long for weeks I rubbed the instrument with the bow producing a horrible sound, wracking everybody's nerves. "Stop it. Stop it!"

"Well, I am learning violin," I would say with an angelic voice.

For several weeks I terrorized the terrorists. Then one morning I found the violin broken. I don't know how. Really. So I was not going to become famous playing Tzigane. I was nine years old and it was the end of my father's dream. Was I mean or was it the first manifestation of self-consciousness? Maybe both, I was already a complex little character.

{ *Translation in Colors* }

I recall with pleasure my long summer days in the park and my long evenings studying English idioms; reading a book in Braille and listening on cassette at the same time in order to learn and correct my pronunciation; bugging Norma with the conditional and subjunctive tense. Obviously everyone at the Lighthouse knew I was an illegal alien. No one ever asked me any questions. It always touches me to think how those people were so open and generous.

Once in a while I worked with clay. It wasn't new for me and I didn't take much interest in it. It was just a pretext to talk to people and improve my English. When Rosalyn came into the class, I was there by chance. "I'm going to do an internship. I am an art therapist. Would you like to come and paint with me?"

"Paint?!?"

"Well, I have been watching you. You dress well. You coordinate your colors so beautifully. Would you like to try?"

"Oh, why not? I want to try everything."

My first painting was an oil in white and blue - just using two colors, I didn't take too much of a risk.

"Did you paint the sea and the mountains in the distance and a sky with stars?"

"Yes," I said, "that's exactly what I wanted to paint."

From that day I began to mix colors together in order to make new ones. I also began to translate my dreams, my moods, my impressions, fragrances, sounds and love and put them on canvas.

I can sometimes see people's auras when they are very close to me. It's sort of a spread of colors around them, sometimes with brown and gray spots, probably the scars of their psyche. I rarely talk to people about it unless they ask. Most people don't like to reveal too much about themselves.

Anyway, hiding from Rosalyn, I made a portrait for her birthday. I entitled it 'Heavenly Rosalyn'. When I gave it to her, she said, "That is my portrait." We laughed. "Okay, you are on your own now." I was already on my own in so many ways.

I took drawing and pastel lessons in different schools. I also participated in two ensemble exhibits and had my own shows in cafes and galleries. I was taking my place among the artistic community in the Bay Area, and bringing my art to Europe and Canada as well. It doesn't matter too much to my ego, but it is important for what I have to say to my fellow human beings.

No need to patronize, to bully, to intrude. We share the same human condition. You can see; I am blind. Does it make me less lovable, less sensitive, less intelligent, less able? I don't mean pitied, I mean really less lovable. I am not disabled, at least no more than any one of us. I could sit on my rump all day or just have coffee and a good time with my friends. I don't have anything to prove, but I have something to say, and that's different.

I painted *Remembrances of Time Passed*. I was an eighteen year old girl reading Proust and patiently trying to explore the feelings of times forever gone. I loved it but whatever I dipped in my cup of tea didn't help me recapture the yesteryears. I was too busy making the present. Besides, my mother didn't bake madeleines and we didn't drink tea. And today I prefer spicy Indian food though I never lived in India. So I don't remember. Images, feelings, sensations, drift like barques upon the eternal current. How many times did I walk on the sandy beach, touch the same tree, lean against the same rock. When was it? Where? In which time? Many times, redone.

{ *Vincent* }

Two in the morning. My daughter Anne's voice on the telephone. A shock. I begin my journey towards death, the death of my son. There are no words to speak of such a pain. Yet images shift in my mind.

Sophie sobbing on the sidewalk in front of the house. Guy, my son's lover, stumbling, supported by two men I don't know. Anne, prostrate on the lawn among the roses, while we await the coming of the ashes.

And I, changed into a piece of marble, a Pieta with empty arms. My own grief set aside to bear the family's suffering. I am there shaking hands with people passing through, talking about Vincent as if he were alive.

Then I feel his presence. He is here with us, the people he loves. Our separation, shaped by a car accident is an earthly reality. Vincent is not gone from our hearts. We are all connected.

My son doesn't belong to me. We belong to the Universal Spirit. I love him.

{ *Encounters with Chagall* }

I visualize a small apartment on the first floor in a quiet street of Brussels, clean with huge windows, a little hall, a living room, a small kitchen, and in the basement an ancient wine cellar, soon transformed into a massage room. Christine, my decorator friend, covered the walls with textured paper. Then she painted it with white lacquer and carpeted the floor in cerulean blue.

The little room was pleasant with a meditative quality. I started to work very hard there, all by myself. It wasn't the blue cave yet. Maybe it was just a prefiguration.

I remember one Friday afternoon it was raining in torrents and the two last clients of the day had canceled their appointments. I was discontented with everything. I sat on my bed and turned on the radio. They were announcing an interview with Marc Chagall. Okay, why not, and I began to listen. And while I was listening to this 87 year old man, I felt a big energy shift. Chagall talking about himself, brave, enthusiastic, full of fun, brilliant but also a spiritual being. For an hour I was mesmerized. This happened in 1973.

That day I didn't know I was going to become a painter. But something in me changed deeply. I remember the voice and the words of Marc Chagall as one of the high moments of my life. He was so present. Then, in the middle of 1986, a few months after I started to paint, I had my first dream about Marc Chagall.

In my dream I am in Paris getting on the big belt train. I am at the station and a woman is screaming, "Mademoiselle, mademoiselle, hurry. Marc Chagall is waiting for you on the train." I begin to run and I feel lost and then someone directs me toward a compartment. The place is almost empty, just a man sitting at the window.

"Come here and sit across from me. I'm Marc Chagall. I have brought a picnic; hard boiled eggs and cheese sandwiches." I am intimidated. "Yes, while the train is going along, I'm going to describe the landscape and we can talk about colors. But first we have to eat. Starving artists don't necessarily make a good piece of art."

I woke up smiling. What a dream, you crazy woman. A few weeks later, I gave a pastel to Miles for his birthday. It was called "Castle in the Sky." The pastel is still in his kitchen. People who see it say "This reminds me of Chagall's *L'Opera de Paris*".

A few months later I had another dream. I am also in Paris, or rather in the Bonne Lieu, in a little bistro where people are dancing. It is summer time. A man comes to me. I don't recognize him. "I am Marc Chagall. Why don't you dance?"

"I'm not in the mood."

"Well I understand. Why don't we go outside. There's a beautiful Lily pond. Maybe we could meet Mr. Monet."

We go outside and the garden is magnificent.

A year later came the last dream. I am painting in a room with a very small window. There is dimmed light, just like in my studio. But I am struggling with lilac and lavender. Suddenly I hear footsteps. The man begins to talk and this time I recognize him. "Hello, Mr. Chagall."

"Hey, what is that struggle?"

"All these shades of purple and violet and mauve and lavender and lilac."

"Oh well. I'm going to explain something to you. Just come here and sit in this high chair. I'm going to take a pillow and sit on the floor."

I am indignant. "Master, you can't sit on the floor. You sit on the high chair."

"No, listen to me. If I sit on the high chair, my students are going to lift their heads and they are going to feel tension in their neck. So they are going to lose their focus. If they sit on the high chair, they just bend their heads gently and listen to my voice. Now you listen to my voice. Purple is red and blue. Lighten the red with white and make it pink and add a little blue and a little more until you feel that you obtained the lilac color. Now look, now put some white in the blue, but let it still be intense. Take the pink and add slowly until you feel that it's enough to give you the lavender color."

"Thank you, Master." I am shocked.

He laughs. "I am Marc Chagall, Good-bye."

I feel very shy, "Good-bye."

I woke up and prepared my brushes and my colors to go to the painting class. When I arrived I told Rosalyn something very strange happened to me. I told her my three dreams about Marc Chagall. I don't remember what she said. She was impressed about something but for a long time I didn't tell anybody. I told Miles and I told a few very close friends. I was very cautious. Is it time now to talk about it?

I'm still not sure. Probably I'm afraid that people will try to make it a big thing, "the channeler of Chagall and blah, blah, blah." You never came back into my dreams. I guess you understand my concerns and respect my space. Marc Chagall, I respect you. I am not your channeler, I don't need to intrude but maybe I am one of your friends from earth.

Pond at Sunset

Sleepy water still blue sky
Suddenly a red sun
Burning brief in bright explosions
Cosmic trance
Then the sky softening
Makes the pond reflect
The color of your soul
Tranquil turquoise
Mystical purple
A smooth silver cloud
Frames the rose hue of your face

Twilight comes tiptoeing
To change the landscape
Into a moody realm
Where long shadows
Slim dancers of the night
Leap across the horizon
Darkening the peaceful dusk
And the place where we live
Secluded castles
With mirrors deeper than oceans
To the end of time
The beginning of no time
With our eternal connection
Now shaped into separateness

{ *Limitations of the Visible* }

Fabian was angry. "You always cook a delicate dinner and I am obsessed with food. I love your conversation but, in fact, I don't want to be here."

"But then why did you come?"

"I don't know. I don't want to be here."

"Where would you like to be?"

"Dead." He threw a glass on the floor and got up to grab something else from the table. I turned off the light.

'What are you doing? I can't see."

"Well, we are equal now."

"We are equal? No, it's unfair. You can find your way in the dark."

I rushed to the telephone and called a cab. "Fabian , a taxi is on its way. You are going home." Anger was gone.

"Give me my coat, please." I helped him, led him to the door, and turned on the light on the stairs.

Before walking downstairs, he stopped, turned toward me and said, "I'm sorry for the evening. I am a depressed man. For twelve years I was in psychoanalysis. I did bio-energy and other things. I am worse than ever."

I remained silent. The taxi honked. "Good-bye, Fabian ."

"Good night." It was 1:00 am. I closed the door, cleaned up the mess and went to bed. *I have played his little sister of mercy for too long. It's over.*

In the morning he called to apologize and began to talk about his wife and how miserable he was. I let him speak for a while. Then I said, "Fabian, I am not your therapist. I can't do anything for you. I guess we are better off separating. Let's not see each other for a while."

Over the telephone I felt his despair more than I ever did before. I felt the pain and cries of sorrow. It wasn't easy to meditate and I chanted for an hour to bring my mind to a place of peace and clarity. It was difficult work and I was physically tired and emotionally exhausted.

At night, I prayed and meditated. I heard a vibration, music, bells, crystal glasses. I couldn't figure out what it was. My body was tingling and very hot. I was sitting on the floor on a pillow. I thought that I was shaking. Then without knowing it, I was in bed, a relaxing sensation invading my entire being. Was it the peace of death? I fell asleep.

The morning noises woke me up. It seemed that my senses, like invisible rubber bands were expanding, expanding to the limit of the unknown. Did I love this man? To be honest, I think that I was only infatuated with his needs.

I am fire and the fire burns. I am water and the water drowns. I am air and the air turns into strong wind. I am earth and the earth quakes.

Was it the message I was sending to men in order to free myself? Women know that fire warms the hearth; that water brings life into the house; that air regenerates our blood; that earth is the secret mother sustaining our steps and nourishing our gardens.

A man showed me his own image in the mirror of his soul. I am a woman. I bear within me the four elements of life. Singing with Anne Bolyn, "When I die, I will give my heart to the fire, my blood to the water, my voice to the air, my body to the earth"…and my love for you to the great universe.

There will be no boundaries. Separateness will become an illusion. Why did I fly from San Francisco to Brussels? Perhaps to gather a missing memory. But I am back with my entire being. Friends are calling me from Belgium, Canada, New York, Paris. I love them and I call back in spite of my telephone bills. I am here in San Francisco. My ladies are here: Olivia, Jennifer, Amira, made of sweet stuff, wide awake, alive; so are the guys with their beards of wisdom, and so are you, rubescent rose glowing in the heart of my heart.

{ *Sequence* }

It was Sunday night. I was walking on Sutter Street, hungry. At the Residence Club, we didn't have meals during the weekend. I had only $2.50 left, just the price of a wonton soup. A woman sitting on the stairs of the Methodist church called out, "Do you have any spare change? I haven't eaten for two days."

"No," I said as I passed by. I wanted to get my wonton soup. I took a few steps, went back and gave her a dollar. Well, she has to eat, too. It's not even a fair share, whatever she wants to do with her money.

I went to the Chinese place and asked for a soft drink. Someone touched my shoulder, "Would you like to eat something?"

"Oh. Oh, no thank you." I thought he was the waiter.

"You are my guest. I would be delighted to buy you something."

"Well, thank you. In this case, the wonton soup." I came back to my room with $1.50 in my pocket and wonton soup in my belly. That's what you get for sharing your prosperity.

{ *Windblown* }

San Francisco wind. San Francisco fog. It's summertime and the
living is not so easy. I'm telling you. That's why I'm going to New
Orleans, at least for a little while on vacation, to get warm in New
Orleans. Free ticket, free house with Kevin and Roy. I fly and here
I am, sunny, hot and stormy. I feel renewed. Is it a new love affair?
Am I going to divorce San Francisco?

One day we went house hunting in New Orleans. You can buy a
home with almost no money. *Could I live here?* I think so. But I'm not
sure.

And now I'm back, back in San Francisco. Back to the fog, back
to the hills. Back to the friendly people, back to the open city, my home
town. San Francisco, my love. No, I didn't betray you. I was just sick
of the wind. Can't you stop it? I guess you can't help it. That's just
the way a relationship goes. You love almost every part of your loved
one except for god knows what. San Francisco, without the wind, our
relationship would be a honeymoon from moon to moon. But the
wind allows our boat to sail. And we travel and we sail and we sail
around and around the bay.

{ *Gypsy Parade* }

Am I doing it again? Yes, but this feels different. A few times in my life I made jewelry; earrings, necklaces, wooden beads, ceramic beads. But in New Orleans in the French market, she was selling beads, glass beads from India, Java, Czechoslovakia, from everywhere, but especially from Africa. Venetian trading beads of colored glass exchanged for gold. More than five centuries of greed. Toward the end of the thirteenth century the Venetians became masters in the art of bead making. They would blow beads which incorporated powdered glass of many different colors.

Kevin introduced us to Anne. "She's a beautiful black woman", said Roy. She was wearing a great hat, a great hat indeed. History, colored in glass beads. I was fascinated.

"Would you share a booth at the art and craft portion of the sixth street fair?" Kai and Jefferey kindly asked me.

"Yes." I paid my dues and then realized I didn't have anything to sell, just some cards and boring T-shirts, like everyone else. And then the beads invaded my life. I worked. I mixed. I strung, long evenings, long thread, smooth glass, rough glass, round beads and square beads, triangles, cubes, irregular shapes, sliding through my fingers like little ice skaters. Slip along the thread and the necklace is growing and growing in multicolored brilliances.

We left early in the morning in Jefferey's car. I was sitting in the back among the boxes. Vivid memories of Spain, sitting in the back among the luggage in another small car, painfully climbing the mountains of Murcia. At the fair we unpacked, covering the table with white linen, hanging, hammering, stapling, taping.

Another fair. I've done so many of them; Marseilles, Paris, Brussels, Liege, and many other towns. This is a street in downtown

San Francisco. Cool breeze, amiable feelings, people dancing, singing, playing music, smiling, talking to each other. "Are you going to make some money? Is it worth the hard work we did? The energy and time we spent?" We didn't make any money but it was worth the day of fun.

Like a gypsy I presented many things; T-shirts, cards, little sculptures, pastels, small paintings, and of course beads. Kai asked, "Are you going to sell something?"

"Well, we're going to try." The important thing is to be here in the street where people are, kids and grown ups. Here they are easy going, unpretentious, fully aware of their community, their rights, their goals.

The kids remind me of little Vincent. When he was five we took him to see the famous Russian clown, Popov. I've never seen a child laugh so hard. Vincent loved street moods and carnivals. He would have been happy here today.

I went to Takilma, Oregon on vacation. It's a community where some of my friends live. There I was drumming, swimming, hiking, dancing. But when I came back the wind, cold, and fog were still here. Dammit. I can't stand it anymore. I think I am going to move to Ashland. But here I am with my new computer, trying to learn the language of the 21st century, stringing beads during breaks. I don't know when I will have the time to paint, but I'm not worried. Time will come.

This is a little summer poem for Robin called 'Yellow'.

Yellow the smoky fields
Fire flaming the mountains
Dry is the grass
Ochre the ground

We live in a yellow tent
We listen to yellow bird songs in a yellow heat
All around the yellow jackets buzz incessantly
People scream
Jump in the river
The river conceals gold among the rocks
Evening falls upon us softly darkening the yellow sky
The smoke becomes invisible
The acrid odor remains
Reminiscence of a yellow day
The gas lamp fills the tent with light and mosquitoes
The first cricket begins its yellow tune
Screechy voice of the summer night
Robin sleeps wrapped in a yellow robe
Midnight midsummer night dream
When Tatania walks dreaming
In her midnight yellow yellow dress

The place is Cedar Gulch. We are lost in music. I'm playing the flute. I can't stop. I follow the drums, the rhythm's got me. Or maybe I've got rhythm. Someone is calling. "Hey guys, back to reality."

What is reality? A prism? A bottomless well? An ocean? An infinite sky? Where is the reality? When a writer makes up a story, they call it fiction. I like to call it invented reality. How many realities can we count? Probably realities are legion. Remember the Spanish play, Vida es Sueno? It's my life dream. Am I asleep? Am I awake? Awake until I die?

A few days ago I was whistling one of those silly tunes from the '50s, and I saw the young image of Frederic, who was a doctor friend of my husband's. When I was expecting my first child I wasn't healthy.

I had to lie down a great amount of time. My mother-in-law was fixing meals for her son and inviting him to her house. Home alone, I heard someone knock at the door.

"Oh, Frederic."

"Are you alone? Where's Adrian?"

"He usually goes to get his meals at his mother's."

"And what about you?"

"Well, I guess I just manage the best that I can." I was in bed feeling so weak.

He took my hand and said, "I am going to prepare something for you to eat." But he could only find biscuits and milk. "May I borrow your keys?" Frederic went out, came back with a huge bag of groceries, and prepared a light meal.

"I'm not hungry, Frederic."

"Force yourself a little bit. I will come back tomorrow morning."

Twice a day for several weeks until I passed the dangerous point, Frederic came to fix my breakfast and dinner. We talked. In his family they had been atheists for generations. He was fascinated by the idea of Satan.

"Well, I am not, although I was as a child," and I told him the story of the billy goat.

He laughed. "But how could the imagination of man have produced the personification of evil?"

"How, I don't know. But I think that an idea can take form," I replied.

"I always expect to meet the devil down the hall at night," he said.

"Are you trying to scare me like the witch?"

"Yes, it's probably fear," he said. "The devil is our form of fear."

Frederic was calm, introspective, charming, and compassionate. I felt very close to him. Even after I recovered and my husband was home he used to come over once or twice a week. He also enjoyed playing with the baby and tried to ease my fear of bacteria.

"You keep this girl too clean," he said.

"Yes, but what about microbes?"

"Do you believe in Santa Claus," he answered.

He would also offer to baby sit, urging us to go to a concert or play. After that we never got the chance to become close again and neither of us ever provoked it. He finished medical school and left for Africa.

Every morning I experience the miracle of living. I breathe and inhale - sounds and scents savored within my silent meditation. I have traveled many roads. I have internalized many landscapes. From seashores to mountains, from deserts to cities, I have met many people, rich or poor, unhappy or content, brief encounters, long acquaintances, episodic friendships and long lasting ones. Most always I am fascinated to listen to people talking about their experiences, especially those who have succeeded in keeping themselves alive without complaints.

The political and corporate world use greed and power to control people, to crush them, to categorize them, to robotize them. But people are people. At one time or another, a spark might flash and light a fire in their heart.

Who is this elderly woman dying of cancer? It's my friend, Lily, a loner with no family and few acquaintances. She spent several months at the hospital where she finally died. I used to visit her there twice a week. One time I found a mobile of seven fish made of straw painted in the seven colors of the rainbow. We hung the mobile in her room. It was so light it moved all the time.

Another visit I bought her a plant for which I've forgotten the name. It was red during the day but the other side of the leaves were green. At night when the leaves were closed it was green. Red daytime; green nighttime. She was enchanted. She also noticed that when someone opened a window the mobile moved faster making the noise of flapping wings. Lily told me, "I wonder if you are aware that you are always bringing me things with color and movement and sound."

"No, I'm not."

"Well, you find a way to keep my senses awakened, open to life." I got the message. Giving is first sharing who you are.

I am sitting in front of my open window. It's a late summer night. The neighborhood is quieting down. Presences surround me; people I have known, people I have loved, those who have passed away, and those who are maybe still alive. They are here around me indistinctly, invisible ties to the great universe. Outside of my windows from closeness to distance, San Francisco, the promenade city with its neighborhoods, its parks, its little cafes, the beach, the bay, the ocean.

When I was little I could see things when they were moving and according to their lightness or darkness in color. I could also see reflections in mirrors and windows. The doctors told my father that I would lose this bit of sight when I reached nine years of age. So my father showed me reflections all the time, teaching me about transparency. He would take a crystal glass and fill it with milk. "See it is different. The milk is white." I could see the crystal glass becoming opaque. He showed me reflections on soup cans and on all things that could catch the light. At that time he was a jeweler and he showed me the reflections on a diamond ring and other precious stones. And that leads to another story.

On my tenth birthday, my father gave me a small diamond ring known as a solitaire, because it has only one diamond. At the end of the summer I came back from the country with infected legs caused by insect bites. My legs were swollen and looked like red pumpkins.

The treatment was very painful and I didn't want to scream or say a word. One day it was more painful than usual and I bit into my ring so hard that I swallowed the stone. The diamond must have been very expensive, because for one week I couldn't leave the house. I couldn't even be alone in the bathroom. I had a special little pot as if my shit were made of gold. I felt very humiliated that my poop was more important than my welfare.

They never found the diamond and that was my revenge. I wonder if the diamond is still inside me somewhere. When I am cremated they might find a little drop of light in my ashes.

I also had an expensive pair of gold earrings that the boys would pull on all the time. "It hurts," I would cry, but they didn't care.

I told my mother, "I don't want to wear those earrings. The boys pull my ears all the time." But nobody wanted to listen to me. One day I took off the earrings. It was hard. They were tightened by a little screw, but I succeeded. I threw them in the toilet and flushed them down.

'Did you take off your earrings?"

"No, I lost them."

"That's impossible. You're lying."

"I lost them. I told you. The boys were pulling on my ears all the time."

" I want to know the truth. What have you done with your earrings? We don't need a little liar in the house."

I stood up, came right in front of my mother and said, "Do you really want to know the truth, mother? I threw them in the toilet and flushed it." It was such an overwhelming confession that I don't even remember if I got punished.

The Prince of Magic Music - acrylic on canvas, 1987

Lady of theWorld - acrylic on canvas, 1991

My Lady of Shalotte - acrylic on canvas, 1995

Storm of Light - acrylic on canvas, 1989

{ *Springtide* }

The sea is playing shuffle board. You can hear the pebbles roll at the bottom of the ocean. There are luminescent fish, immense forests, and high mountains moving with the Springtide in the equinox winds - hidden kingdoms of Mother Earth where caverns and deep valleys keep the secret source of life.

I dive down to the bottom of subconsciousness. The plunge seems infinite. Did I live 20,000 years? Your companionship helps me to drift with the Springtide without sinking, bringing to the surface all that needs air, light, and space.

Here is Ocean Beach in the fog. We walk along in the crisp air, coming back through Golden Gate Park. How many times? Extant of exaltation, silent walking meditation, talking, sharing, breathing.

I get out in the misty morning and go sit in Buena Vista Park, wrapped in a soft cloak of fog. Brusquely, the sun brightens. I feel flooded with gold. Stories rush through layers of memories, swirling like a jitterbug dance. Each one wants to be told, heard, pictured, smelled, tasted. Here I am, deciding, choosing, discriminating.

I remember a very peculiar one. When I was five I was very small for my age. Petite, they said. I was running with a group of kids, racing on the sidewalk along with the bus speeding in the middle of the street. I tried to keep up with the others but I was left behind. All of a sudden, I was three meters in front of them.

The kids shouted, "Hey, you trickster, you can't do that. It's not fair. You flew above our heads." They started to push me and drag me by my coat. Some grown-ups at their windows yelled and came down.

"Stop it. What's happening down there?"

"She's a cheater. She's a cheater. She flew over our heads." The kids were all talking at once.

I heard my father's angry voice. "Get away from her you bunch of dirty bastards. Leave her alone or I will knock you out right on the sidewalk." He sheltered me in his arms and took me home.

The following day he questioned me. "What happened yesterday with your little friends?"

"I don't know. I felt dizzy, but I didn't fly. They're lying. I'm not a bird."

My father stroked my hair and laughed. "They say witches fly across the sky on a broom stick. But that's just superstition."

I found the word funny and I repeated it. Superstition. What could it mean. I chanted a long time - superstition, superstition, superstition, skipping noisily around the house. Then I forgot about the word.

{ *Sister Sarafina* }

When Sister Sarafina arrived in the neighborhood she made an attempt to civilize the kids. "We're all going together to a little house with a beautiful garden."

I liked her. She played piano and let me sing solos in the little choir. I thought that she loved me very much. One day she said, "You have the face of an angel. I would like to teach you to pray."

During the evening dinner I told my father. "Sister Sarafina is very nice. She wants to teach me to pray."

"Who is Sarafina?"

"She's a nun," said my mother. "She came here about three months ago. She brings the kids together and lets them sing and play games, teaching the little girls how to knit and sew."

"Incredible. And you let our children go with a nun?"

"Well, all the kids are going," said my mother. "And this little one is alone all week. It would be good for her to mingle with the other kids."

My father was calm but very determined. "But do we need a nun to teach our children how to live? I'm going to talk to the mayor, today."

And then Sister Sarafina disappeared.

{ *Mirage* }

Lost in the desert, blinded by sand and sun, we looked for a green oasis. It's there. We are approaching the village, the well, the palm trees. But where is it? Gone, the mirage, the spring. Jacom Boehm said, "The great secret is to walk in all things contrary to the word."

Once I knew a kind man who confused growth and spirituality with excitement and drama. "I want to share with you," he said, but there he was jabbering, jargoning, intruding, crossing boundaries.

"I want to share with him, but there is no place," I thought.

Along my path I have found true friends. Magnificent. I glorify the spirit of man and rejoice in being a microcosm of the vast universe.

Song to Myself

I celebrate a newborn day
For I am alive
I celebrate my health
and my strength within
I move and dance and sing and breathe

Music in the morning
when breakfast preparations
bring the scent of coffee
and toasted bread all around me like a promise of good omens

I celebrate my way to love
every little misfortune
and good fortune
Celebration is my daily sunbeam

I celebrate my own beauty my hair of silver silk .
glowing in the morning breeze
I celebrate my kindness to people
my gift of colors and light
imagination and freshness
within the dream of friendliness

I praise all things given to me
and praise my life ardent and free
I praise my past and my present
I praise today and tomorrow

I celebrate my coming death
and I respond to all.

{ *The Crystal Tree* }

This book was instigated by Carol while I was in bed with a broken knee. Was it part of the healing process? My fast recovery? Writing may be one of the answers. The attention and the support I received, your presence in my home, my strong desire to enjoy life again, to stroll under the sun, to let my body sing the mystery of my own being. All these reasons made me healthy again.

I recall when I was five years old I had a very strange illness. For three months I didn't get out of bed. Every week I was taken to the doctor who gave me painful shots. At first I screamed and fought. Then I lost my energy. I was in and out of coma. Everything was lukewarm, insipid. But, I knew I wasn't dead. I realized that I would come back again.

One day my father pureed a potato in vegetable broth and tried to feed me. In the evening, our neighbor, the witch, came in. She took a bowl, filled it with water and rested it gently on my head. In the bowl she poured a teaspoon of olive oil and began to stir it with her middle finger.

"Not even my five fingers can mix the oil", she said. "Someone has cast a spell on this child."

My brother, Paul, came and placed candles on either side of me. The witch performed a ritual for a long time, saying prayers in a language I didn't understand. Three days later I got out of bed, but I had forgotten how to walk. My father supported me and taught me how to put one foot in front of the other. Later my mother related the ritual to me.

We never knew what kind of disease it was.

{ *The Tranquil River Of Her Fever* }

She listened to the silence of the night, the murmur of the night, its voices. Footsteps and laughter of unseen strollers; rustling of tousled hair, her own, or the dark hair of the night hiding as intangible spider webs.

She sails upon a tranquil river on which sleeps the melancholy of her town. She heats the strokes of time from the bell tower of her sadness; little girl aware of the last breath of the last spoken caress of the last dream of water, of flowers sending smooth pebbles of perfume, bearers of memory.

The children burn the dead leaves of the chestnut tree. A big pile of which rests underfoot, giving off the odor of a village. The children throw on newspapers, dry wood, kerosene; all that flames and crackles so that the fire gets high. Virulent.

Then the backyard fills with smoke. The children are thrilled with the acrid smell which makes the nose sting, the eyes tear, the throat scratch. They laugh, shriek, circle around the fire. The kids now think of themselves as dangerous arsonists, hunters lost in the jungle, soldiers on campaign, bivouacking, facing the enemy; cavemen laying on the ground waiting for an easy prey and discovering the fire; the great god keeping away wild beasts and evil spirits and the dead creeping among the shadows.

Was it yesterday? This morning? Was it a game? A dream...

The little girl looks for a cool spot between the burning sheets; she trembles and wrinkles like the leaves of her vision. The backyard, the night, the room where heat dampens an endless fevered agony. How long the hours of tangled time and duration. And life. What is life? A thread, a question?

123

A living notebook - my father used to say: "This little girl has a clock in her brain. She's never late. She always wakes up when we have to leave early. She always remembers the things that we have to do during the day." I hear his voice, "Little girl tomorrow I have to get up at 5:00 in the morning. Would you wake me?" or "I have to see a new client at 1:00 Thursday." and so on, and so forth. How did I know it was 5:00 or 1:00. I never wore a watch. Did I feel overly responsible?

Every night I would go into the kitchen two or three times to drink water and I was very scared. I wrapped my blanket around me covering me from head to toe. Each bit of my skin had to be protected. In my soft blanket, I felt safe. I tried to wake up no one but I probably did because sometimes I walked in my sleep without my soft protectors. I did strange things, like turning on the stove burner, standing up on the window ledge or climbing up on the pantry shelves. In the morning my father would say, "Do you remember what you did last night?"

"Last night? I did nothing." But when I went to the boarding school, it stopped. I had learned to sleep well. I am not such a notebook anymore. But when I need to wake up, I can wake up at any time. I sleep well and I don't feel responsible. But I guess an angel is calling out to me "Hey you, it's time to get up."

Now I have a clock and a watch. Since I bought them I have lost a little bit of my sense of time. But I seldom use the alarm. When the heater begins to make noise, it's 6:30. When I smell the strong sense of coffee from my neighbor next door, it's 7:00. When the man upstairs comes back from work, it's 4:00 am. Voices, sirens, starting cars, people's habits, and the city life tell you the time. But also something else, I just can't explain. Sometimes, people ask what time it could be. "Oh, maybe 10:00." We look at the clock and it's ten to 10 or 10:05. I like to use my sense of time. I notice that watches and clocks make you feel impatient, sometimes restless. But don't be late, said my father, a king is waiting for you. "What king?"

"Everyone is a king." So I told him, "I am a king too. I can be late sometimes." But since we are all kings, princes, high priestesses or whatever I carry my watch in my purse.

Today while Mary is doing reiki on my knee, I see a five-year-old struggling to get her strength back. Why did I want to leave? Could it be that I knew about this moment? Is it possible that we have subtle knowledge of a future latent in our subconscious mind?

Roses, orchids, stalks, so many flowers in the room make me slightly uncomfortable. Is this my grave? I laugh. No, these flowers are the symbol of friendship, support and love. Food, gifts, encouragement these are hugs or whatever each has to give. Familiar voices sing songing, whispering, crossing my sleep; remote footsteps, a squeaky door, the rattling of the dishes in the kitchen. Why don't you write about your life? Boring. What about some vignettes? So among many I chose this mixture of bitter sweets for the love of you, you who knows more than this book could ever contain.

For my father I was a rabbit; for my mother I was a mouse; for my brother, a dog; for my teachers, a mountain goat. But now I am a hawk. I fly high. I dive fast. I grab what I have seen from above. But vision is not necessarily discernment. I don't predict. I don't prophecize. I channel, at times. I am always squeezed between the burning Sagittarius and the secretive Scorpio, harmonizing fire and water. Maybe that's one of my purposes in life. Or maybe, I don't have any purpose at all.

The walls of my house are covered with paintings. Who are these spring seasoned princesses, these ladies, these goddesses, these musicians, these pilgrims? Where are they coming from - the ponds and the mountains, the flowers, the forest, the sunset; these abstract images of lines, circles, geometric forms, shapes and colors? People ask me, how do you know the pond? How do you know the mountain? And, how do you know the sea? I know the sea through the sound of the waves. I know the pond through the scent of the silent water. I know the mountains through the winter descending from the glacier. I know the sunset through the iris of your eyes. I know the light through the prism of your soul reflecting in me the colors of the rainbow.

I don't do visual art. I do reflective art. If I touch you and size you up, if I smell you, if I hear you, if I taste you, I sense your body inside of your aura. I surrender to the pleasure of being in a human dream. That's you becoming diaphanous figures in my paintings. You are spirits; essences; fairies embodied in flesh and blood; the manifestation of feeling, passion, emotion, movement.

I was sitting by the River Meuse sharing a joint with my friend Mila.

"Life is a roller coaster," she said.

I may have been in a Cyrano De Bergerac mood that day. "Life can be anything. You can visualize any infinity of images. Life is a rotten apple, a prickly bush, a damp basement without windows. Challenging, life is the climbing of a steep mountain, a long hike across a rocky canyon, a weight lifted. Cutesy, life is a fragrant bouquet of pink and blue flowers, an army of new age angels flying around your bed while you are asleep."

"Stop that. Tell me what is life for you."

"Well, it's just life. I wouldn't be very original if I tell you that life is a journey."

"I take your images but a journey to where?"

"Probably a journey to myself."

She sounded more cheerful. "The fog is lifting. A bit of blue sky is showing above the water."

"Mila, let's be silent for a while." A barge passed by. Hardly audible, the fog horn echoed its deep sound over the landscape. Two verses by a French poet jumped from my heart: 'Good-bye old River Meuse. You are like a lullaby. Good-bye, Meuse, so sweet to my childhood.' That wasn't my childhood. It was my kids' childhood. The fog hung over the water, dripping of sadness.

Mila broke the silence. "Yes, life may be a journey to myself, but I refuse to travel." I shivered as she spoke. "You are a good pilgrim on a pilgrimage toward the absolute."

"I am the wind. I received my share of pesticides but I survived."

"And you will be like the wind. You are not afraid of change. You will find joy over the ocean in new cities with new people."

"Is it a prediction, Dr. Gypsy?"

"Yes, Doctor, but I am Gypsy no more, unfortunately. You are a strong and courageous woman. You undertook the most perilous, journey to yourself. So, Josée, Bon Voyage."

The Kingdom Of Spirit Is Embodied In My Flesh

A single white rose
The clear sky above
The path up and down
Trampled by heart's desires

There is a killer on the road
Always a killer

No matter where it is
Where you are
Just travel your own journey
There is an angel on the road
Always an angel
A single white rose
Priestess of the morning star

The boat on the river
Can take you to the sea
There is light on the road
There is love on the boat

Don't let it pass you by.

From my room I hear two fog horns answering each other, one low, one high - the ocean and the sky. San Francisco is in slumber, wrapped in its blanket of night. I wonder how many people lie in bed awake just as I am.

Image from the past or a visitation; I see Walter and Inga traveling arm in arm across the river of remembrance. I can visualize very well the time and the place.

Good Pope John had a dream: to assemble all the Christian churches with their similarities, their differences, their liturgies, their music into one peaceful, loving family - heaven already beginning on earth. My husband and I were fervent activists in the Catholic avant-garde movement. The first ecumenical convention took place in the little town of Verdun. All the streets were filled with people arriving from many different countries. There were Orthodox Greek, Prot-estants of all sorts, Calvinists, Lutherans, Methodists, Baptists, and of course, Catholics. Meeting people was a great pleasure. There were talks, lectures, forums, group exchanges, and also a lot of sharing. For the first evening dinner Walter and Inga sat at our table. I wasn't especially pleased, a German couple. Well, they have the right to be here just like me.

We started to speak cautiously about the decoration of each table, the room, the environment. Walter volunteered some information about himself and his family.

"I am a psychiatrist in Munich. My wife is an interior designer. We have three kids."

"We have a little girl," said my husband. "I am a college professor. My wife is a psychotherapist."

We talked about schools, children, about methods of education with the kind of excessive politeness used when the brain is masking the heart. A question was burning inside of my mouth. I wanted to get it out. "The psychiatrists must have been very busy during the war. Were you already a psychiatrist?"

"Yes, I was."

"So, you might have known a lot of things - concentration camps, medical experiences…"

"Obviously I knew some, but not as many as you might think. And I disapproved of them."

"Oh, you did. Well, did you speak up to denounce the crimes of your dictator?"

"Unfortunately not."

"Do you know that they killed thousands of Jehovah Witnesses, millions of Jews, homosexuals, communists, anarchists, free thinkers, gypsies, artists, children?" I felt hot. My face must have been as red as fire.

"We didn't know then. And now we are sorry."

129

"You are sorry, huh?"

"We didn't get much information. We heard vague rumors. But how can someone imagine such a horror. I am a pacifist and nonviolent. I always admired Ghandi. Do you think that we Germans are all criminals?"

"So far, I do. For these times of doom even silence is a crime."

"Yes, but look at the United States with McCarthy, the witch hunting, and the Rosenbergs who were made to die.'

"Yes, it is very sad, but you can't compare that to what the Germans did. It's beyond human experience in history."

So we talked, missing a few lectures and a big part of the festivities. We couldn't stop talking. We learned to love and know each other. Since then many German people have crossed my path. Some of them became my friends. I could tell them about Sarah, Margaret, those times of suffering and disobedience, but I seldom do.

I remember my father talking all the time about his war, talking especially when we had guests. That was his one-man show, a mixture of landscape descriptions, horrible events, jokes, happy resolution, stories about women - most always ridiculed. Most days I was so bored of his nonsense talk. In my heart I made a promise - if I have to witness a war I will never talk about it.

Am I breaking a promise? What is this all about? Five years through which an adolescent struggled everyday to become a young woman, unbroken by the bombings, starvation, inequities, and the chaos. Of course, I am breaking my promise. I broke it years ago. And so, God bless me. I care not for World War II. I outdistanced armies, parades and battle fields, but as I go along the line there are other challenges and sufferings. I am strong. Yes, I am vulnerable. This is my life. I am not ashamed anymore to be. I am not afraid anymore to love.

130

{ *Mila* }

Mila was beautiful, not a beauty for magazine covers or a TV fashion show. She hardly wore make-up. My daughter Sophie portrayed her this way: hair like a summer night, eyes like puddles in the wood reflecting the green of the trees; and a heart as good as ginger bread. And so many more things which I can't explain - bright, sweet and strong. Mila was gifted. She had an enchanting voice. She would compose music and write songs and poems. She entered many contests to make money and always won. But the most important thing for her was her work at the Geriatric Hospital. She was a doctor. A few months after her death, one of her supervisors told me that in her department, the patients lived longer, recovering their mind, feeling great joy and pleasure to still be alive.

She had talked to me about her astral travels. Sometimes at night she visited her dying patients in order to help them go peacefully. She didn't want people to know about it. Many of her clients spoke of having seen her come into their rooms by their beds in the middle of the night when they felt frightened and lonely.

Her parents were poor immigrants - her father from Yugoslavia, her mother from Czechoslovakia. They both worked hard but remained poor as they raised two children. Mila was bright and decided to become a doctor. A priest we knew very well helped to pay for her tuition. On weekends she worked in restaurants and nightclubs in order to pay her rent and save herself from starving.

A young journalist from a well known conservative newspaper fell in love and wanted to marry her. For seven years he pursued her incessantly. Finally she accepted and Paul became a possessive and despotic husband.

"I made a mistake, Jo. Why did I marry him? Why? I didn't love him really. Security? Tired of being poor?"

"But Mila, you are a doctor now."

"Yes, but I work for the city. My parents are getting old; I am helping them, and I have a loan. I have so many debts from when I was a student that I don't know what to do. I let myself fall into a trap like a mouse. I'm a caged bird - the wife of Mr. Paul Lambot. But soon I will get away."

"Don't we think we are all living in cages or behind walls?"

"Probably some cages are bigger than others with more space, more sunshine and fresh air. But they are cages so what difference does that make? I knew when I married that I sunk my sense of freedom and identity at the bottom of a well. I didn't even want a glimpse between the bars."

Meanwhile, almost every Friday night I was singing and playing music in a jazz club. The Roture was small, cozy. The musicians could get free drinks and appetizers. We usually played until four or five in the morning. One night around 1:00, the bartender called out "Jo, telephone."

"Oh, who's calling me here?"

It was Paul Lambot. "Take a cab, come right away. Mila attempted suicide. This is the third time. I can't stand it. She wants to talk to you." He was yelling. I thought he was going mad.

When I arrived at the house she was lying on the living room couch. I hugged her and kissed her hair. "Oh, Jo they looked for you everywhere in town. I wanted to see you. I want to ask you a question."

"A question?"

"Yes, do you love me?"

"I love you, Mila. You are my friend, my sister. Please stay with us. The journey is not over."

"I'm afraid that it is going to be over for me. I've had enough of living." I waited until dawn. She fell asleep. Paul was pacing the room.

"You can go home now," he said. "Thank you for your help."

Three months later she finally ended her life. Meanwhile I had moved to another town. I had talked to her on the phone a few times. "We are going to see each other soon." But I never saw her again, at least not in this world. While I was thinking about my clipped wings, she predicted that I would fly. I never returned to the jazz club. I didn't play music again until I came to San Francisco. But many times I did sing for her and for a few close friends. Was she the invisible companion on the path to self realization on my way to freedom? Did she know that I would find my home?

{ *Anastacia, Pantomime* }

I met Anastacia a few times in Andre's groups. So when she called for an appointment, it was very easy for me to picture her, her fairy tale character - the mixture of the Little Mermaid, Donkey Skin in Scheherazade, and just a touch of sugarplum fairy.

We began our first session quietly. She remained silent for a while. Then she exploded, "When I was eighteen my father, a well-known lawyer, tried to put me in a mental institution but he couldn't find a psychiatrist to agree. In spite of his money, he didn't succeed in buying a doctor to get rid of me. I was disobedient rebelling against his ideas, his rules, his behavior. Could he win? At times I was frightened. It was probably in one of these moments of fear that he forced me to marry a young lawyer from a rich family. Six months from my wedding day, I took all the money I could and escaped to Paris with a new lover. I was still a minor citizen under 21, so the International Police found me and brought me back to my father's home. I waited until my 21st birthday to leave the house. Now it's been ten years. I learned a lot of things: massage, bio-energy. I learned a lot but I am still struggling."

I lightly touched the back of her hand, "And you feel-you need some support."

"Yes, I can't do it all by myself, and I want to grow even if it will be painful at times." We worked together for several years. Now Anastacia is an NLP master. Along the way, we became friends. The friendship still remains.

I remember the first steps from therapy to friendship. Anastacia asked, "Why don't you come to visit. You don't know Ghent."

"No, not very well. I would be pleased to visit."

"I just moved. I have a new apartment," she said.

134

And there I went. We spent three days talking, visiting the city, playing, shopping, going to an Arabian market to buy shiny Moroccan silk. In the evening we draped ourselves with the fabric and got into different personalities, playing out favorite characters, singing favorite songs.

"Tomorrow I have to run some errands for my mother and stay a little while to visit. Why don't you come with me?"

"Do you think it would be appropriate?"

"Oh yes. But beware father is going to ask you a lot of questions about your new life in America. The house is richly furnished but moldy, dark, and full of sorrow. My parents are very uptight."

"Oh, I see. Since I'm leaving tomorrow night, it's going to be the Grande finale."

"Oh no! Just a bore as usual. Just promise me that you won't sigh."

Her father opened the door and immediately dust, darkness, and constraint hit me right in my heart. The salon was heavily furnished, decorated with trinkets and walls covered with ancestors' portraits and ancient Flemish painters' work. Anastacia was describing the room humorously. I whispered, "It reminds me of my mother-in-law's house."

We all sat down around an old table, conversing politely. But the lawyer snapped, "I don't understand how you can live in America. Those people don't have any culture or education."

"What makes you generalize that way? Do you think mainstream Belgians have a lot of culture and education? You know that even in democratic regimes, culture and education are still privileges. All my American friends are well-educated and highly cultured. But if you like generalizations I can tell you that American people are generous, straight forward, open, without class prejudices. And I am always disappointed by the hypocrisies of our bourgeoisie," I thought, I am trespassing the boundaries here. This is a mundane visit. I regained control over myself. "I guess we are not here to do sociological analysis."

The lawyer laughed dryly, sending a cloud of smoke into my face. I coughed. "Certainly not," he said. "So tell us about your life there."

I talked about my writing, about art, about music, and the pop song I was performing just to improve my English. We sang *"Try to Remember the kind of September"*.

Anastacia's father was whistling. Her mother was singing with me. The only quiet one, for a change, was Anastacia. As soon as we got outside she told me, "What have you done to them? I have never, never heard them whistling and singing."

"I really don't know. I probably pushed the right button. The blue one. You know, the good old days when we were young and life was so wonderful."

"Oh shit," she exclaimed. "Don't you have anything else to say?"

"Yes. Let's go have a waffle with fresh whipped cream and a caffe latte."

During my fifteen years as a therapist, three of my clients became close friends. I occasionally socialize with some of them. I always tried to relate to all of them as myself, Josee, a human being and a therapist. I loved my profession. I think I still do love it. But I have chosen a different way of living. It is for me, another time.

{ *The Castle of the Fool* }

I opened the door, Jean rushed in. "The man coming from the rain," I laughed. "Sit down."

"No, I have to make haste. I just came to tell you something. I bought a house."

"You what? Where, how? Did you win the lottery?"

"No, it didn't cost very much. It's practically a ruin."

"What are you going to do with a ruin?"

"Well, it is in the country. We are going to work to make it nice and comfortable."

And we worked indeed - fall, winter, spring, and summer, weekend after weekend. We made concrete, cut sheet rock, carrying sand, bricks, wood, cleaning the land around the house, digging up the garbage that people had buried: horseshoes, pieces of glass, rusty tools. We wanted to grow flowers, herbs, and vegetables. Sometimes, especially during the cold season, I came home with swollen hands exhausted and very proud because I understood that this place was going to be my refuge any time with Jean and Yvon, my friends forever.

Today the house is a gem among the vines and the roses. One of the bedrooms upstairs is called La Chambre de Josée, but it's also the temple of many dreams, many books, many projects. After several years of absence, I came back to the home of Jean the poet and Yvon the healer. Everything was changed, renewed, luxuriance in the garden, abundance in the orchard, long summer twilights, tranquil time of meditation.

I walk around hugging the trees goodnight. I cross the lawn and come back to the simplicity of the house. I sit on the terrace and write a letter to you, a poem for you. Here I may be 'the magic butterfly, the unicorn in the forest.' I savor the aromatic flavor of love. But in San Francisco, my hometown, I am Josée and I love it very much.

I tread on sidewalks, get on buses, work, shop, stop and shoot the breeze with a neighbor. Here I am an artist, a listener, a talker, a lover. Here is Miles and here is Fred. And how many wonders will my city contain? I breathe with the wind, with the trees, with the sound of the waves. I love among its people. I drink the sunlight. I dream in the shade. I dream. I dream that I reach out and touch your heart. Yet San Francisco also has its shadow.

{ This World }

She gets on the 71 bus
Walks slowly toward an empty seat
Ignoring the driver's call
"Miss, your pass."

"Oh yes, I lost it
Sorry
The wind took it from my hand
I think it's in the bay now
I don't know who I am today
I don't know who I am today
No I don't"

The driver seems touched
"Where are you going?"

"Going? Going somewhere
On Market Street maybe
To a place where people learn to dance the 'Can Can'."

The passengers are silent
Her voice like a plaintive violin
Keeps playing its soft lament
As we move through ribbons of fog

"I am lost I am lost
Please God show me the path"

Lost
A woman
Old and young
A child rattled by the tide of life

I search for some comforting words
There is no way
To patch her wound
In order to lessen my pain

I am speechless
A wall
An iron gate
My heart cries for mercy
"But what does it matter to you?"
You are lost
I am shut
Did we really create this world?

{ *San Francisco's Little Miracles* }

Every one of us has many experiences of coincidences, or rather, synchronicity. It's not very original, but if we are open it happens many times, even in one day. But these three little miracles are so dear to me that I can't help telling them to you.

One of my friends came back from Australia and stayed with me for a few days. While we were talking about her trip she let me hear a tape she recorded there. It was a digerido player.

"Oh, I have dreamed of finding a digerido for so long."

"Well when I come back in three years, I will bring you one."

"In three years, that's funny. Maybe I won't be thinking about a digerido then."

Two days after her departure a neighbor came to my door. "You know I was in the park with my husband and we heard a man playing a strange instrument. Since we know that you are interested in all kinds of things, we asked what it was. He said it was a digerido from Australia."

"Yes, I know what it is, but where did he get it?"

"Well, we took his phone number." I called him and asked where he found his digerido.

"I got it from my teacher, Mr. Fred Teigen. You can talk to him. He makes American digeridos. They are good."

I called Fred Teigen. He asked me, "Are you interested in buying a digerido and taking a few lessons?"

"Yes."

"Well, my digeridos are $90 and I also do shamanic work if you're interested. I sell the digerido at half price for my students, of course."

"I have done some shamanic work with a group, and I am very interested in doing it individually."

Then he asked, "Oh, you did shamanic work in a group? With who?"

"With Leslie Grey."

"Leslie, she's my wife."

Unbelievable, what a surprise that I didn't drop the telephone. We made an appointment.

That day the same neighbor came with a big bag of shoes. "Believe it or not I found this in the park."

"New shoes."

"Do you want a pair?"

"Hmm. Not really except if you have a turquoise pair."

"I doubt it."

She poured the bag of shoes on the floor and at the bottom of the bag there was a pair of turquoise shoes. I put them on my feet and they were perfect for me. Very inexpensive compared to what I had seen.

A few days later I bought a tarot deck. I asked Miles, "Do you have a box for my cards? I know that you have just about everything in your basement."

"I don't think I have one, but you always find what you need. We'll see."

"We went for a walk in the park. We sat, and under a bench, there it was: a Chinese wooden box, decorated with flowers and a butterfly, in perfect condition.

If I am broke in the morning, there is a little money for me in the evening. If I am sick in the evening, the fever drops in the morning. If I am sad in the middle of the night, then joy pops up in the middle of the day. Just like the lamp lighter in the Little Prince. "Bonjour, it's daytime. Bonsoir, it's night time." Even when the pain seems intolerable, my creative self comes alive to express music, color and forms.

I don't know if this is a gift. I think it's given to everyone. But I don't take it for granted, I thank... I don't know who to thank... God, the Great Spirit, the universe, the angels. I really don't know so I thank them all. So I think that I really should thank myself for being attentive. Why is it that some days everything seem so easy, everything is smooth, everything works, everything falls into place naturally - almost like magic. Then some other days, everything goes wrong just as if people wanted to make it difficult for you. There's no help, no friendliness. It's really puzzling. Is it a reflection of ourselves? A lack of "positive think" or a state of mind that we are not aware of? How much of that do I do to myself? I'm not really sure.

Am I responsible for the bus being late, for the banana peel that made me slip on the middle of the sidewalk with my grocery bag breaking just as I wanted to cross the street, a shower pouring down just as I planned to eat my sandwich in the park, my landlord twisting the rent control rules just today, a returned letter, a bottle of olive oil spilled in the kitchen and more and again today?

Today I was walking on Haight Street with a friend. A woman was lying on the sidewalk. The police were coming. Three homeless men surrounded her and told her to get up. She didn't want to move. But my friend Barbara talked to her, "Sister, get up. Try to get up." She moved and she talked and she got up.

On Jessie Street

There is no wind on Jessie Street
On the sidewalk people sleep in boxes
The children play 'Kick the Can'
A strong smell of urine sweat garbage drying in the sun
Make me weary

I open up my purse
Find a small bottle of vanilla scented oil
Bring it to my nose
Closer and closer
Until I smell nothing
But vanilla beans
Vanilla cake
I remember during the war
My chubby little mother
Baking huge trays of vanilla cookies
Each time a neighbor or a friend
Would go into the woods joining the Resistance
I hear my own children asking for more
Vanilla rice pudding
I daydream of vanilla flowers
With dancers in the temples of Bali
Offering their scented bodies to the Gods
And the tourists
A glow of fragrant vanilla candies

A crack in the sidewalk makes me stagger
  Oh Jessie Street
  I am walking on Jessie Street
  On the sidewalk where people sleep in boxes
  Children play 'Kick the Can'
  Until they grow up
  And then what?

My city is crying. The homeless are persecuted. The prostitutes on the sidewalk shiver in their raggedy clothes. Kids live on Polk Street trading their bodies for money in order to survive. Home, a dreadful place to be with alcoholic and drug addict parents. Okay, let's build prisons, put more police in the streets and support greedy landlords, big business, hunt the criminals, the street people, the neglected children and cut the education programs. Maybe they will subsidize death squads like in Brazil.

On weekends, and sometimes on other days, new age yuppies come to town. Here they are pushing, shoving, bumping into people. They stop in front of the shops and occupy the sidewalks like empty and heartless cows.

" I hear you and so what are you doing in this country?"

"What am I doing? It's my choice. It's my heart. I trust the magic of San Francisco. I trust the people I love. I trust the artist, the poet, the women's movement, the gay activists, all the friendly citizens awakening a little more everyday. And there are hundreds of thousands and more and more."

The drought is over they say. But I couldn't find the little surge of water up in Buena Vista park. There are daisies and buttercups. The grass is damp but the sun is out. It's warm today. We are sitting by a cedar tree. There are a lot of people lying among the tiny white flowers. It's a gorgeous day. Thank you, San Francisco.

In my childhood, I heard French people saying: Neither fortunes nor misfortunes ever come alone. One day I told Fred, "I'm so late. I waited more than 15 minutes for the bus."

He replied, "I guess we have to have mercy for those kinds of things." Maybe it's one of his little secrets - have mercy for our misfortunes and be thankful for our fortunes and being alive.

Don't cry when I die. Don't come to my grave for I won't have one, but come now to share, to grieve, or to play. Let's taste everyday with rain or sunshine. I don't even know if this life is mine. I know who I am, or, who I am not.

I am here and there. Where? But everywhere. I am the breeze. I am the sky. But there is not I. There is not self. Some Buddhists friends would say, "We are nothing, and so we are everything everyday."

December 13, 1993. This book ends on a rainy night. I listen to the shower harassing my window pane. Soon the sun will shine bringing back the city to her usual mood. But today, San Francisco in the rain conveys boxes and bags of memories from a gloomy flat country where people are strong, serious, and reliable. Faraway I can silhouette a woman singing Bob Dylan in French, "Sad lady of the lowland with a murky mouth in missionary times with her eyes like smoke and her prayer rhymes".

I look at her in the distance under a cloudy sky walking toward me and then vanishing. Hello Josée. Good-bye Josée. Hello Josée. Aren't you complete yet? How many more lifetimes do you think you will need?

146